WISE WILD DIVINE

A COLORING BOOK OF GODDESSES AND SPIRIT WOMEN FROM AROUND THE WORLD

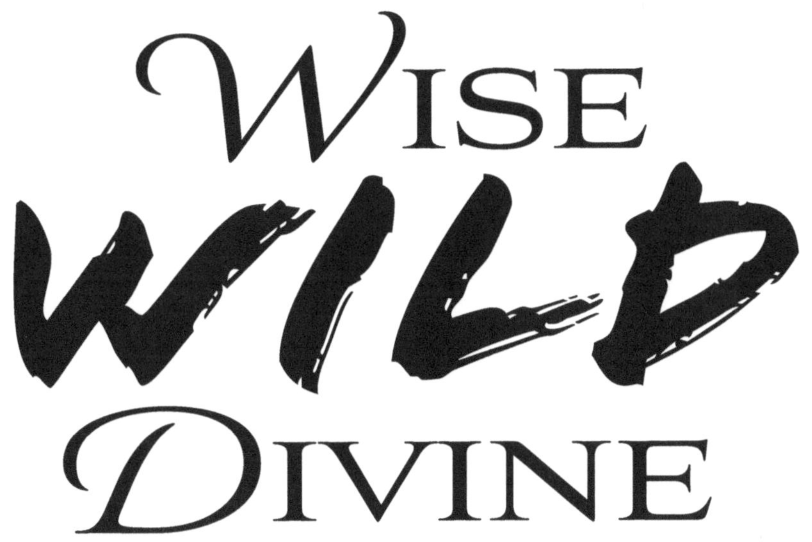

ILLUSTRATED BY SERENA GUERRA

Wise, Wild, Divine
A Coloring Book of Spirit Women from Around the World

ISBN

For my son, Sebastian,
may you always stay wide-eyed and curious.

Special thanks to
Jeff, Daphne, Andria, Jim, Amy, & Don
for without your support this book may still be an
idea in a notebook on my shelf.

The goddesses and spirit women featured throughout this book cover a wide range of mythologies, religions, and indigenous cultures from around the world. While some artistic license has been taken, I've sought to capture the essence and integrity of their respective stories. Their descriptions can be found in the index, and further details can be found online.

Enjoy this collection!

-Serena Guerra

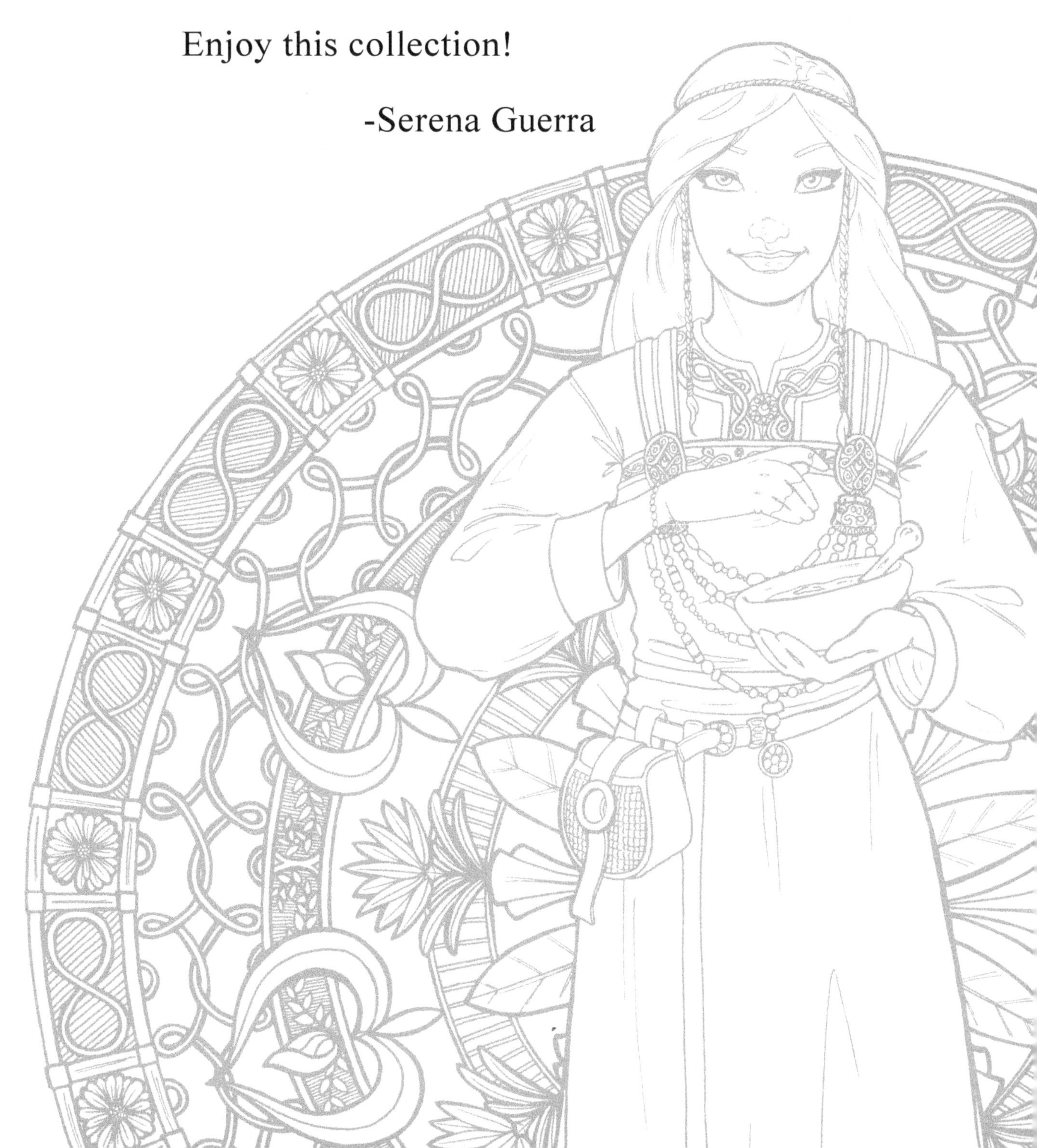

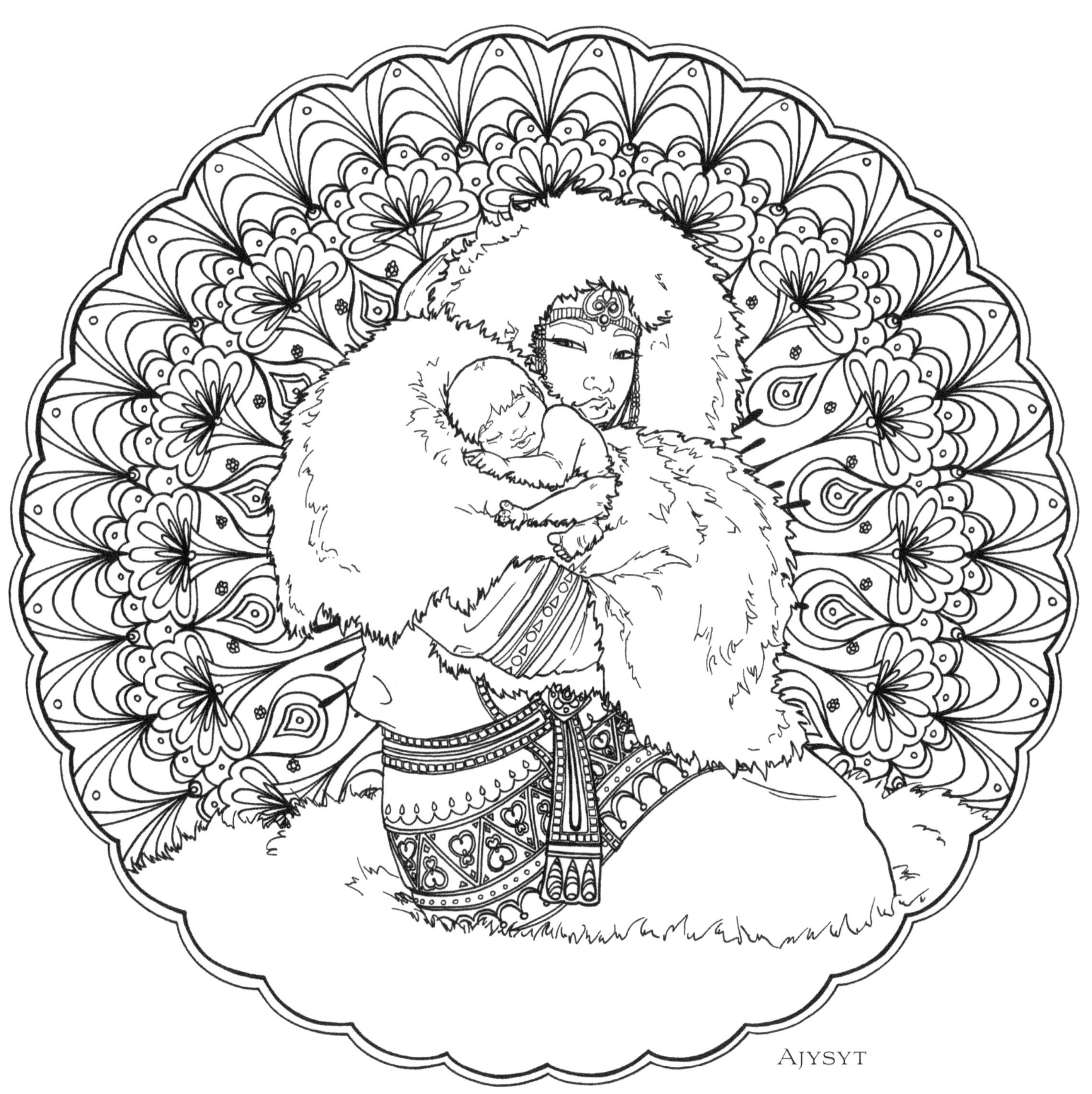

Ajysyt

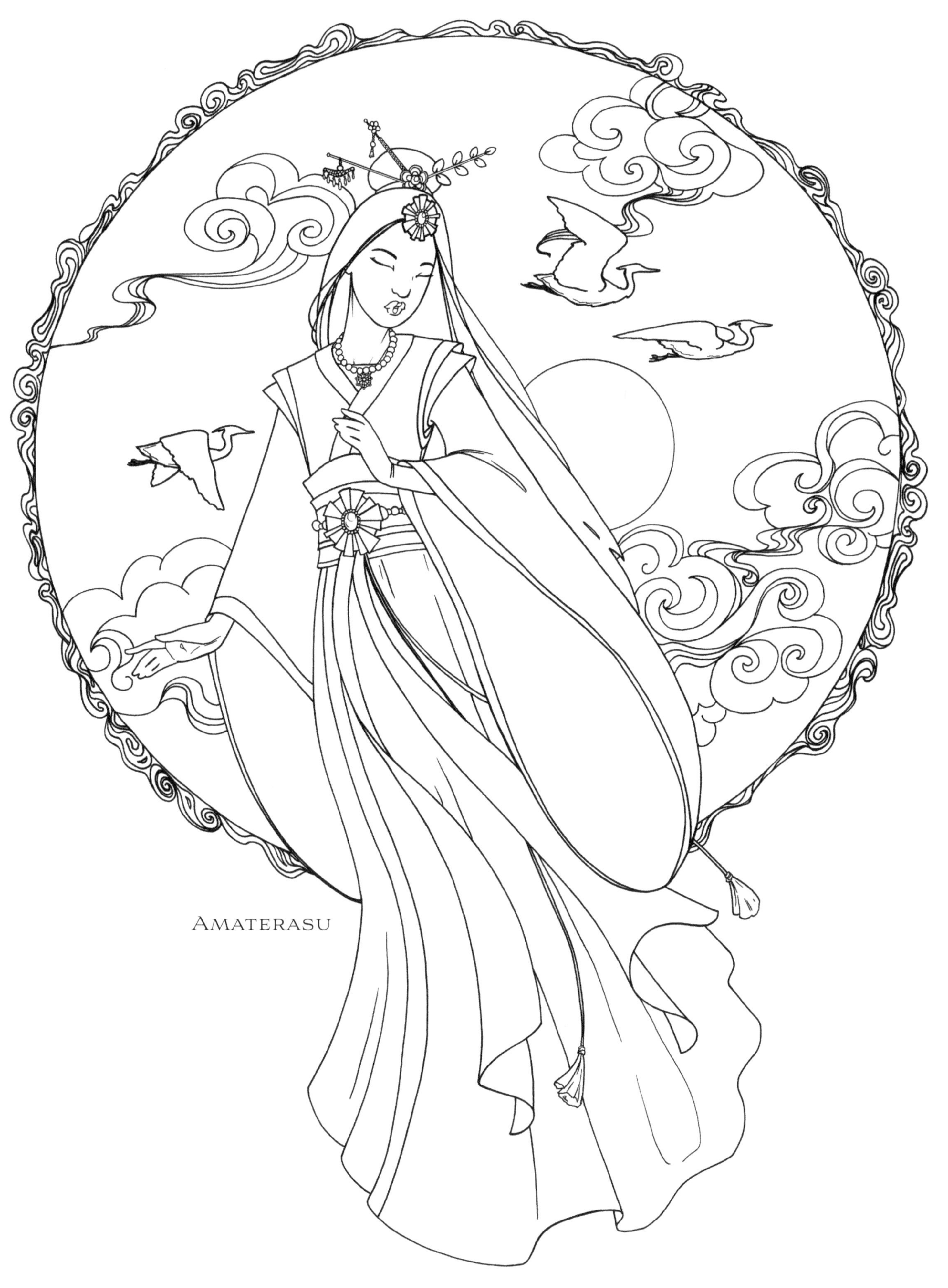
Amaterasu

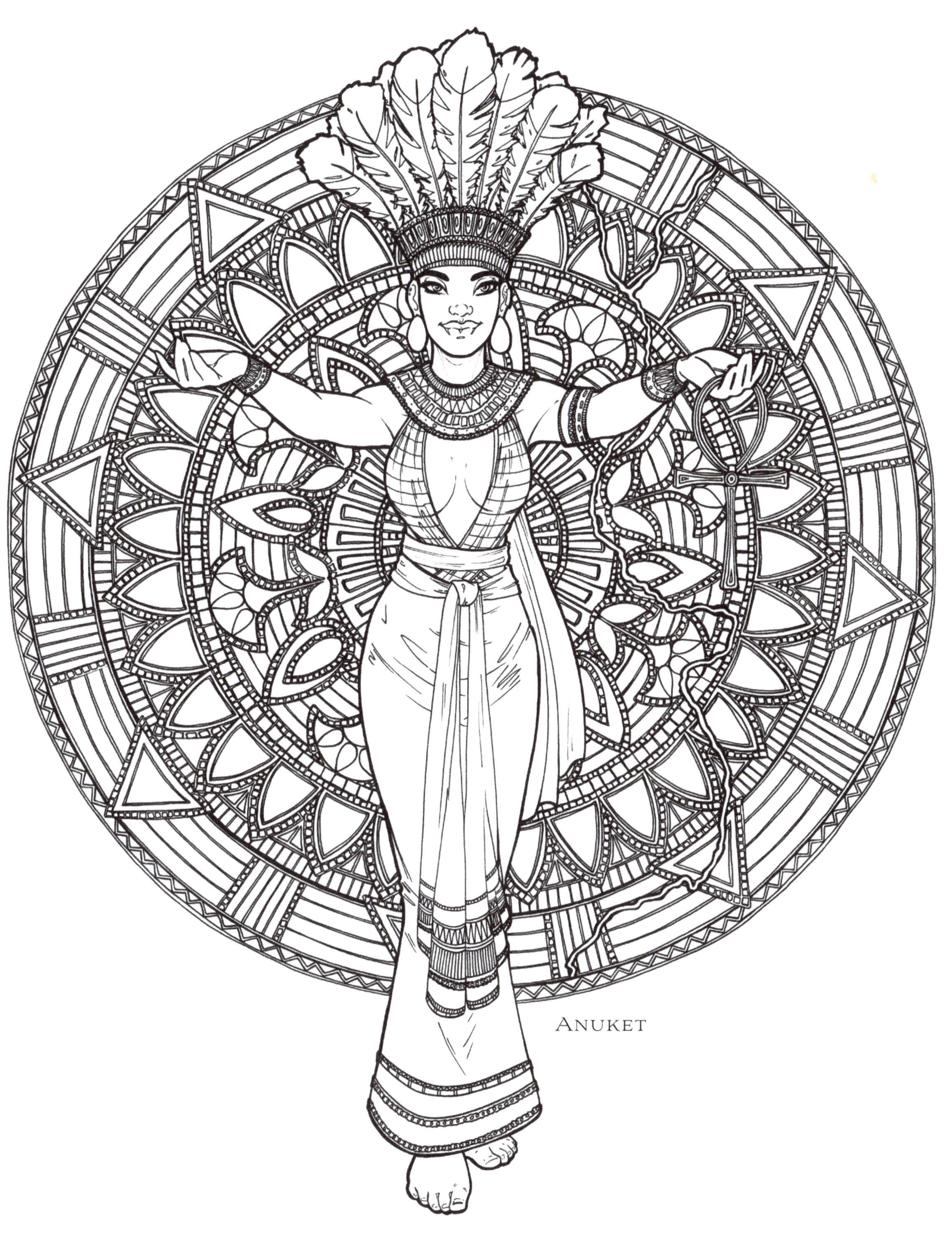
ANUKET

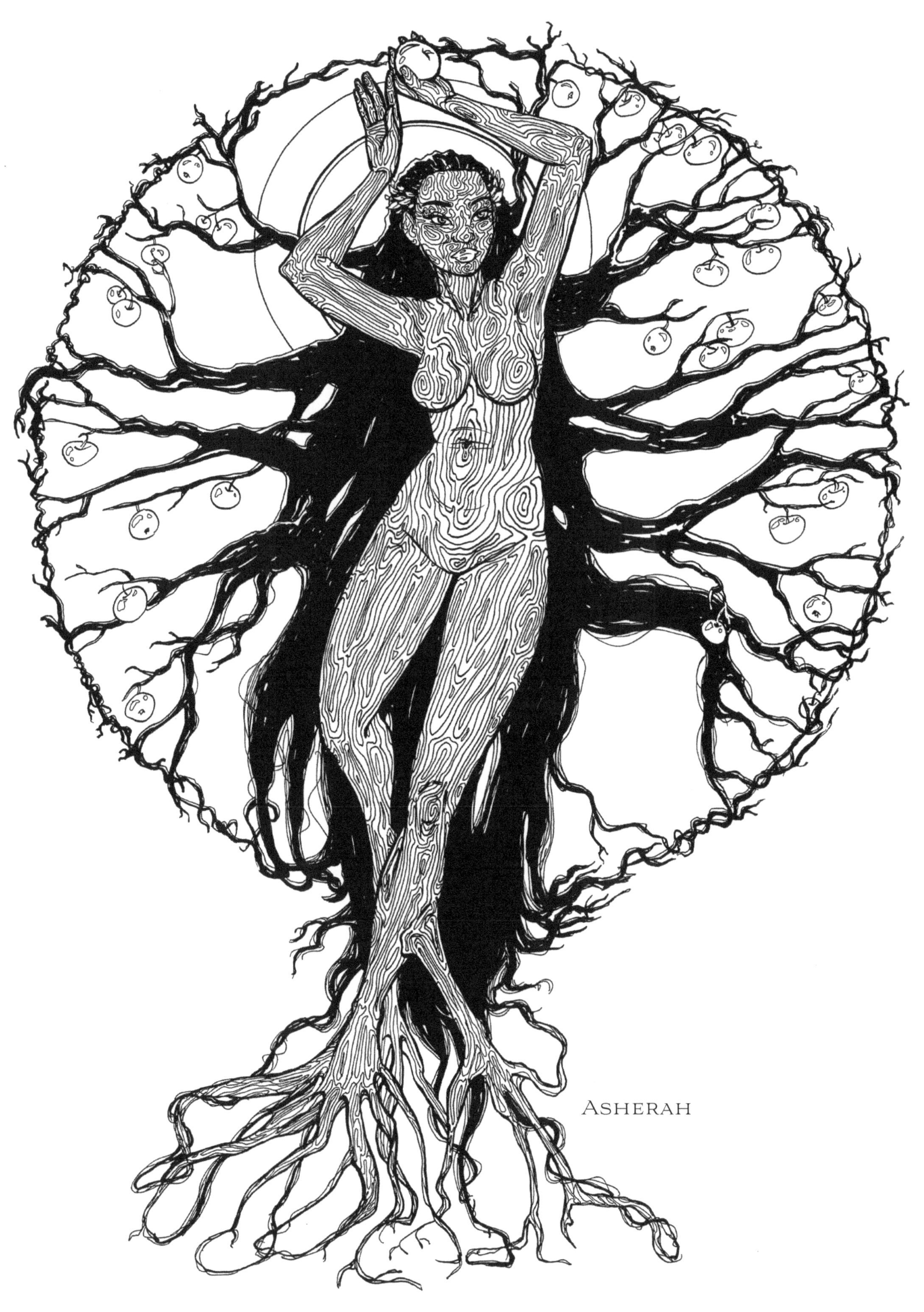
ASHERAH

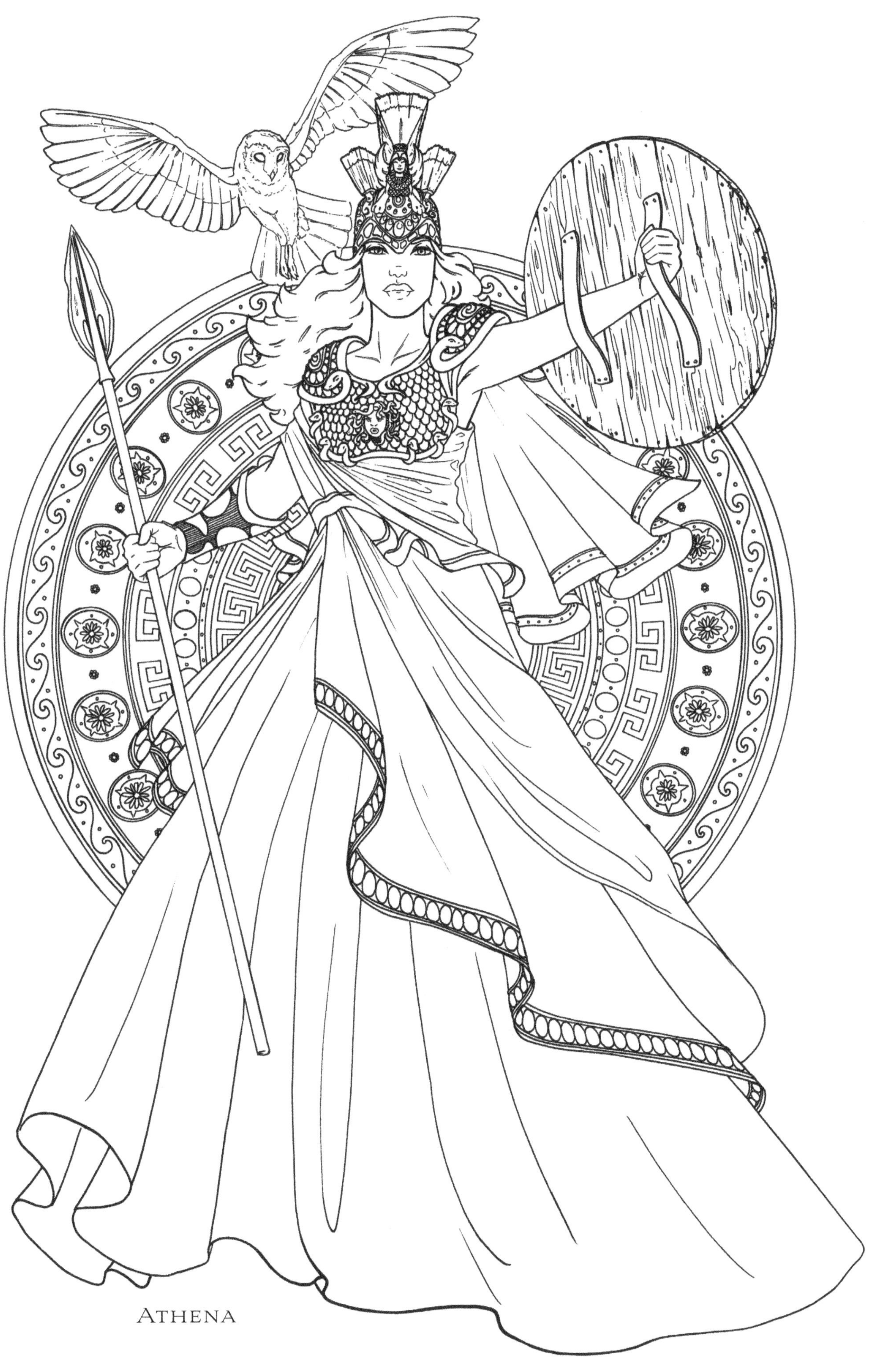

ATHENA

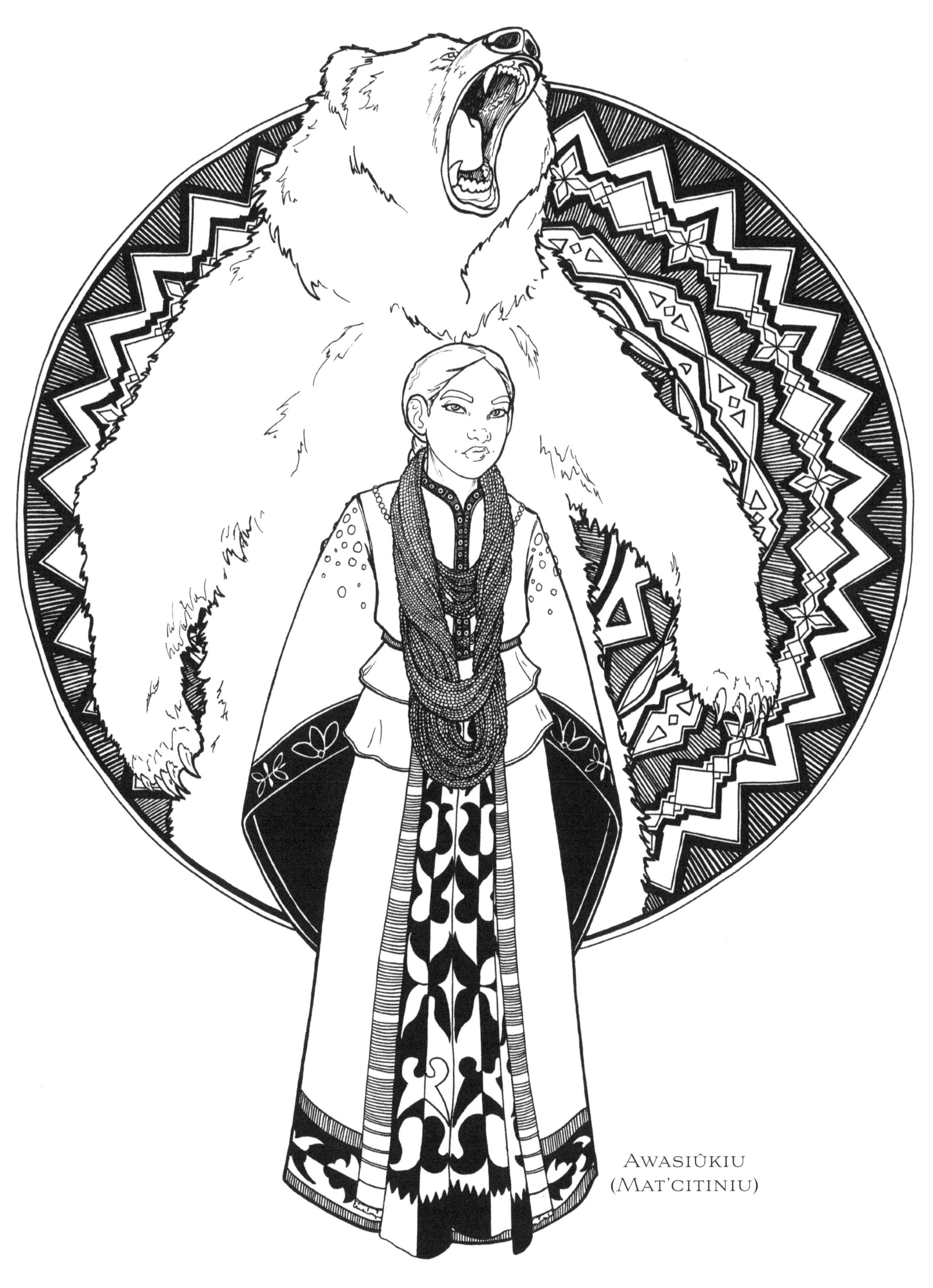

Awasiúkiu
(Mat'citiniu)

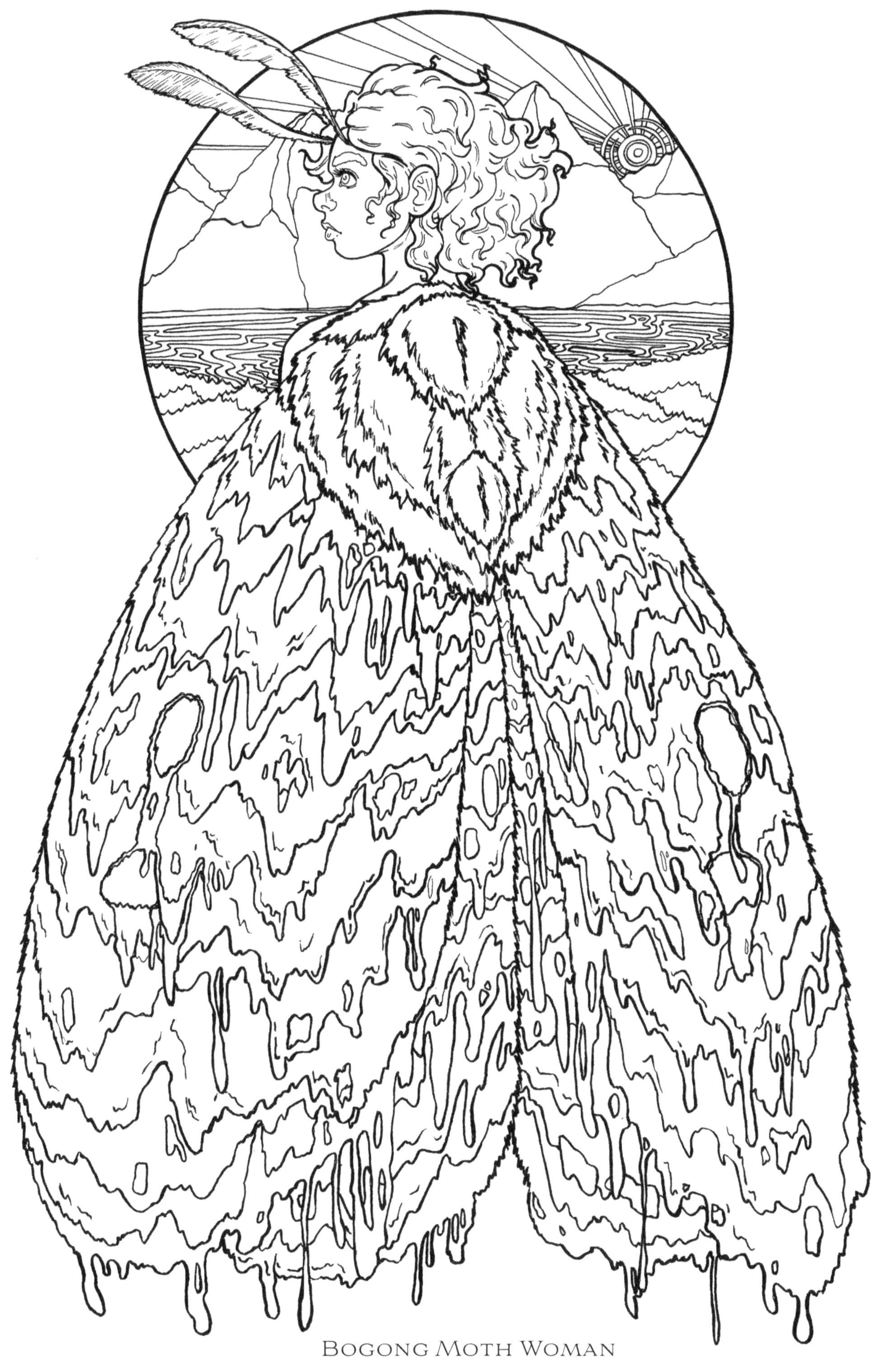

Bogong Moth Woman

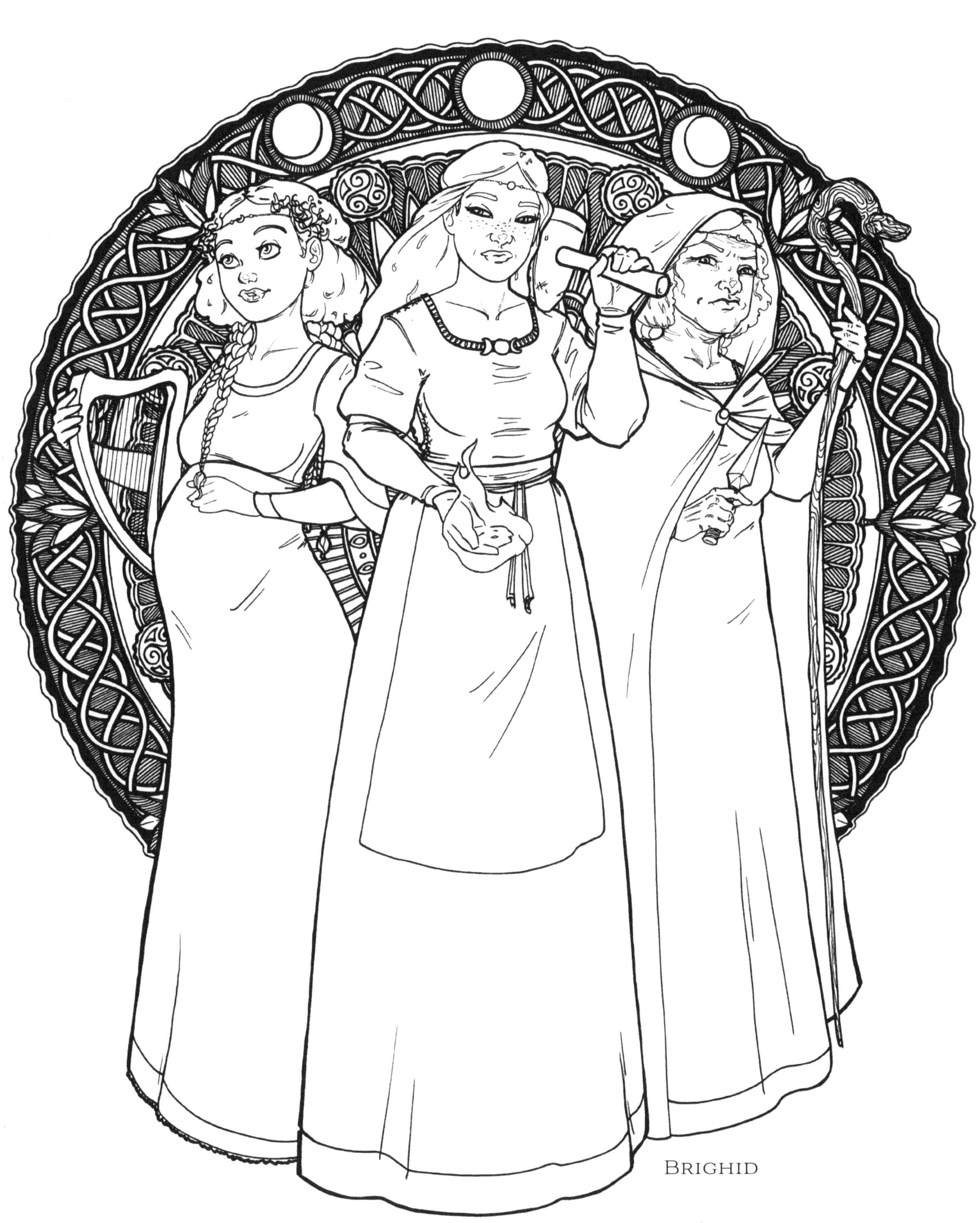

Brighid

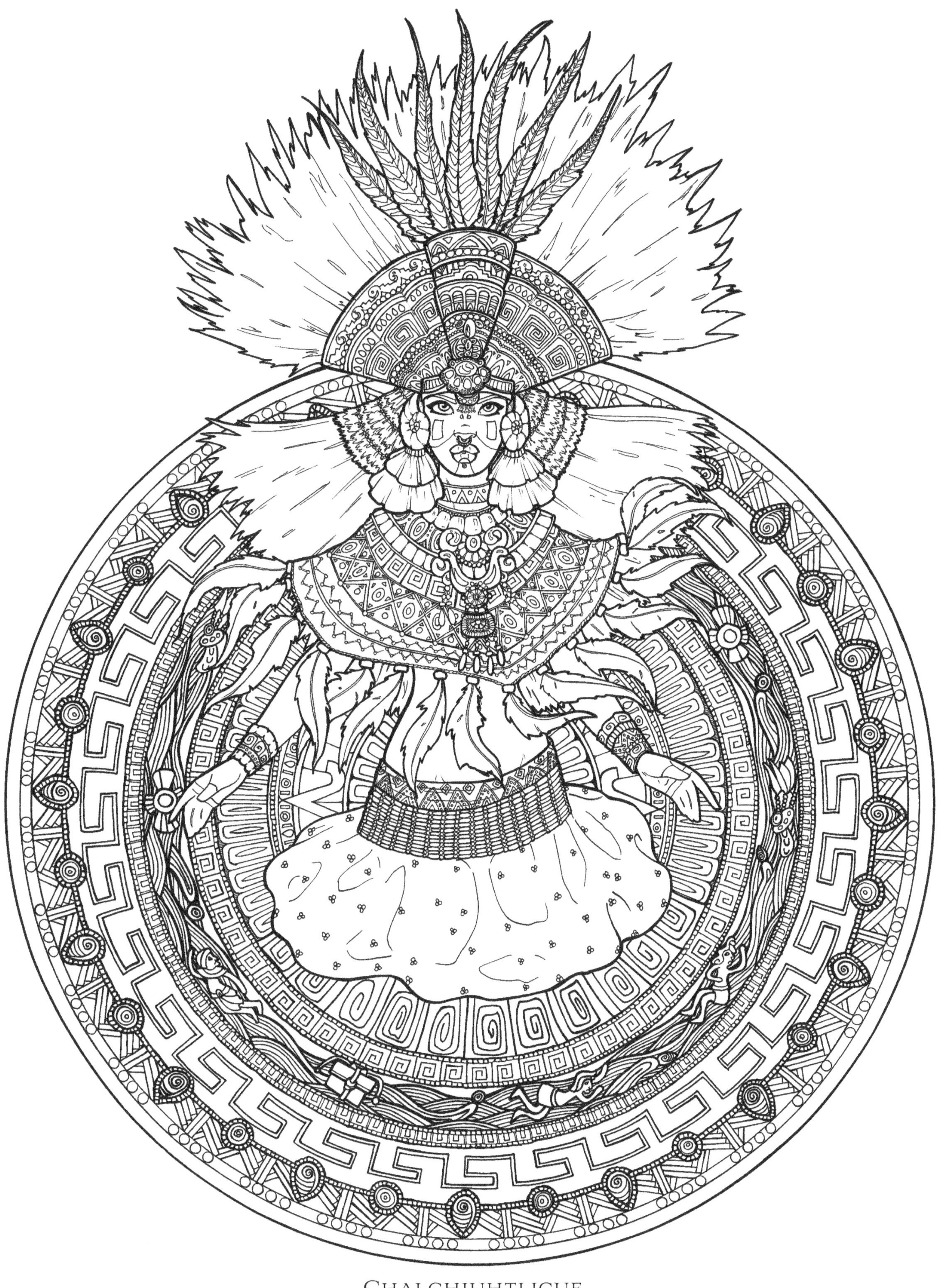

Chalchiuhtlicue

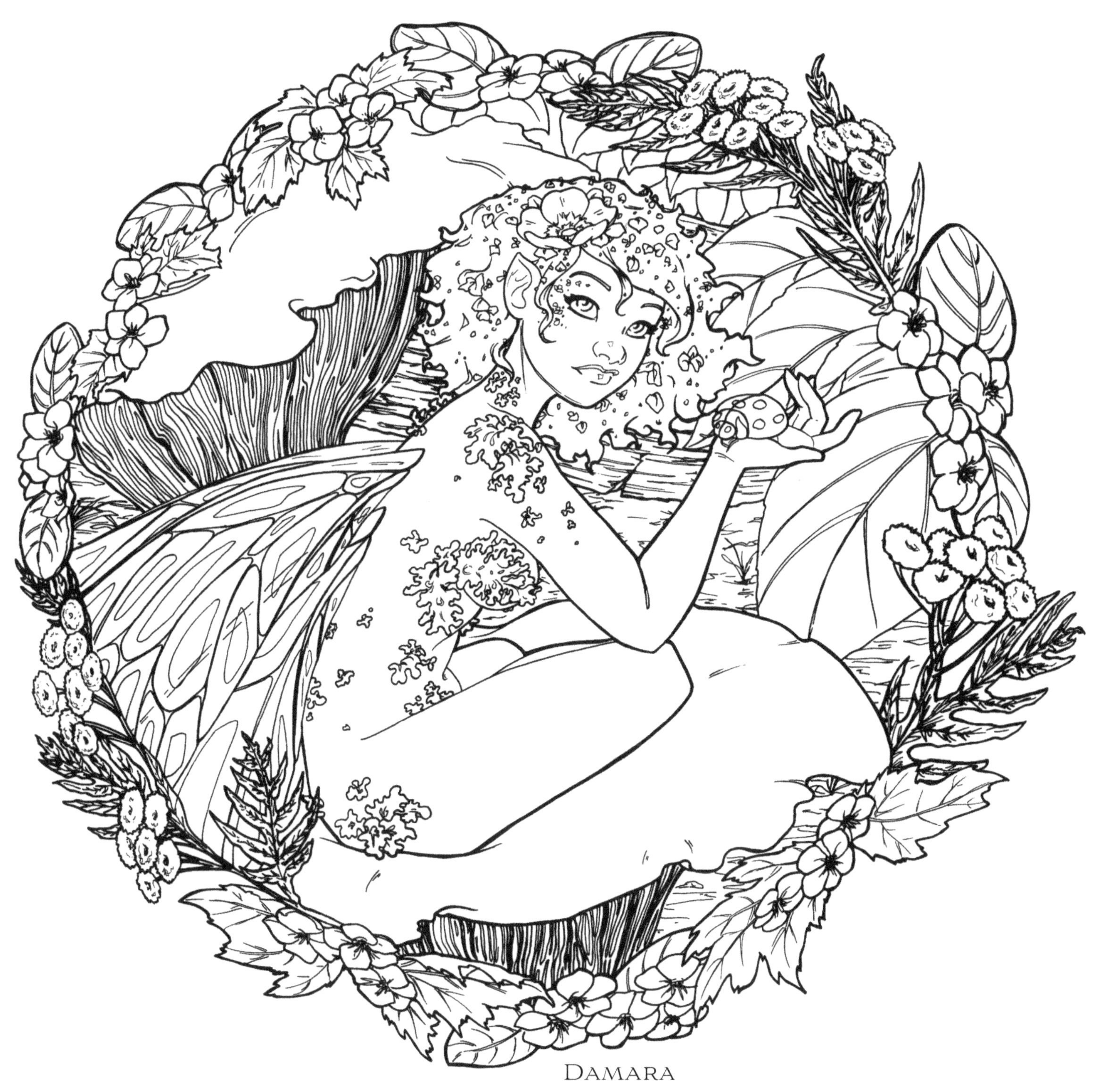

Damara

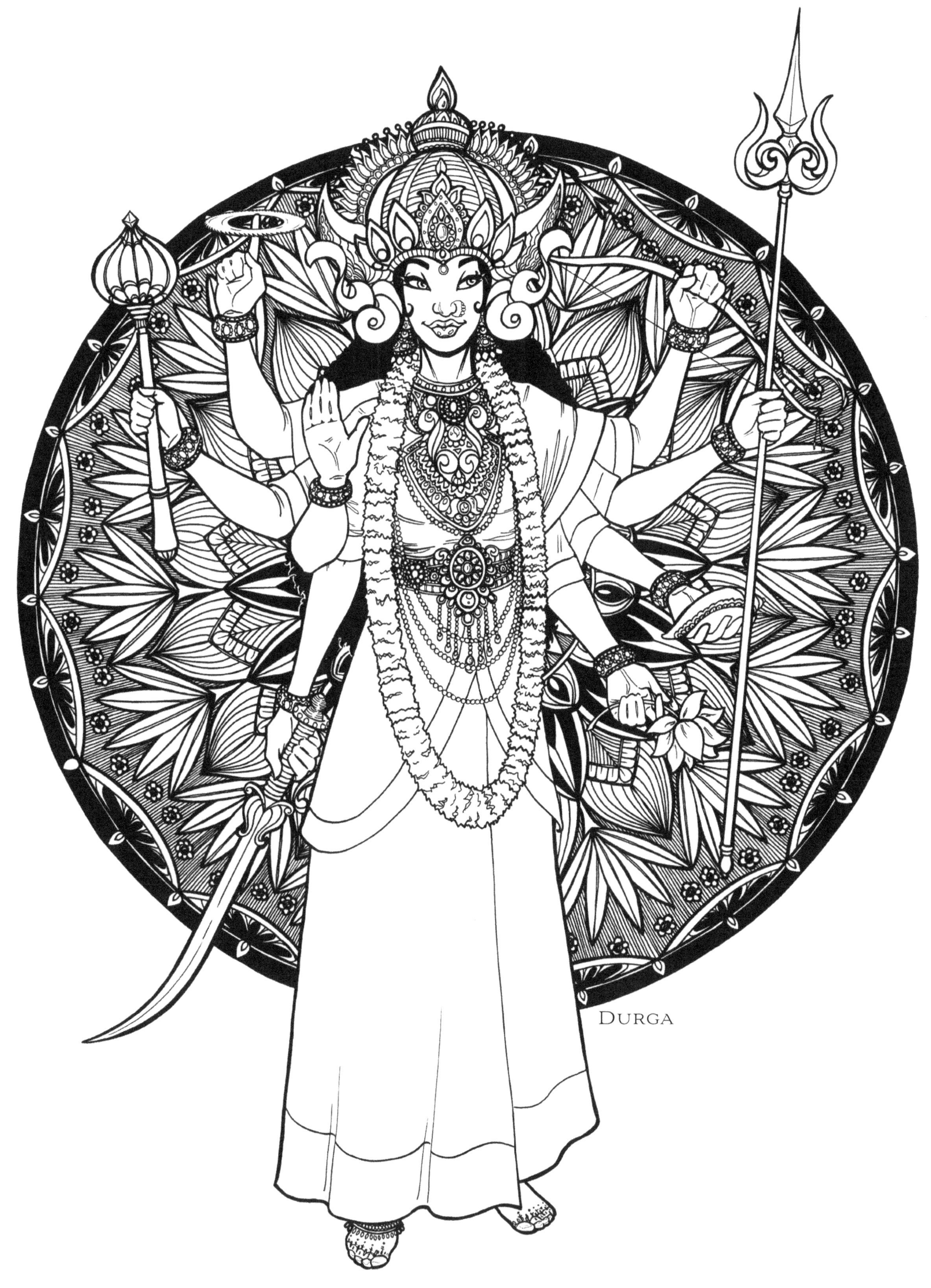

DURGA

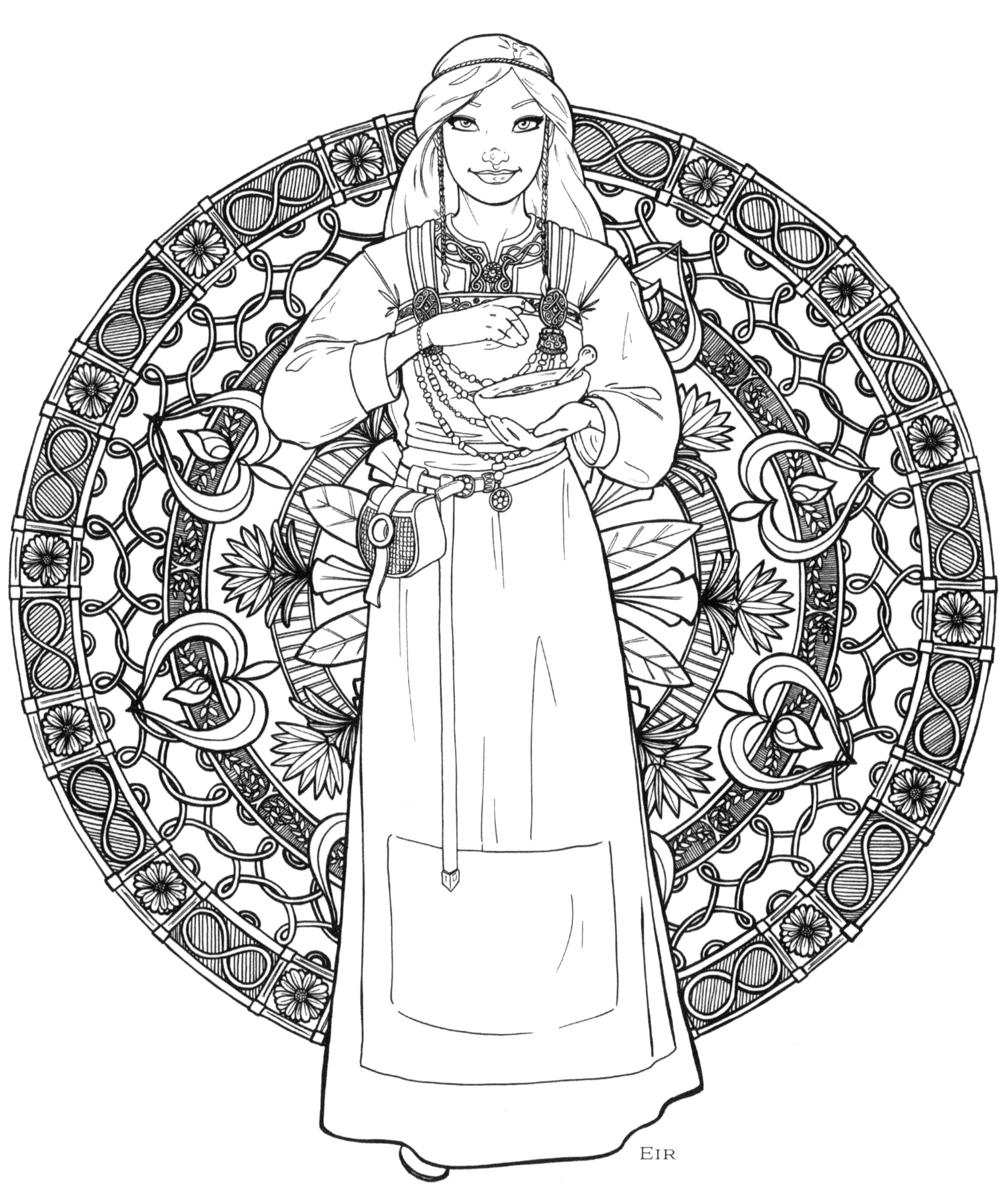

Eir

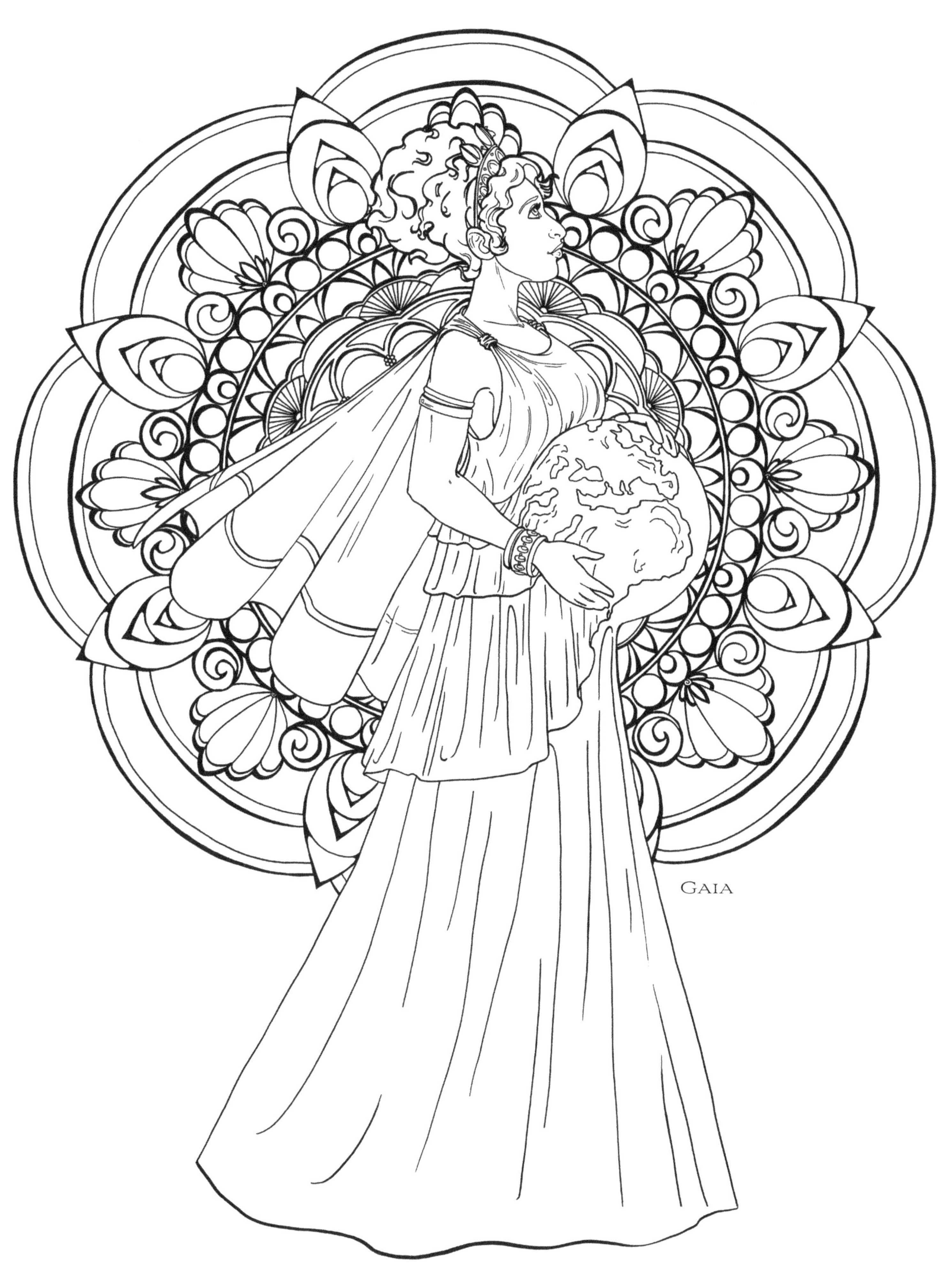
GAIA

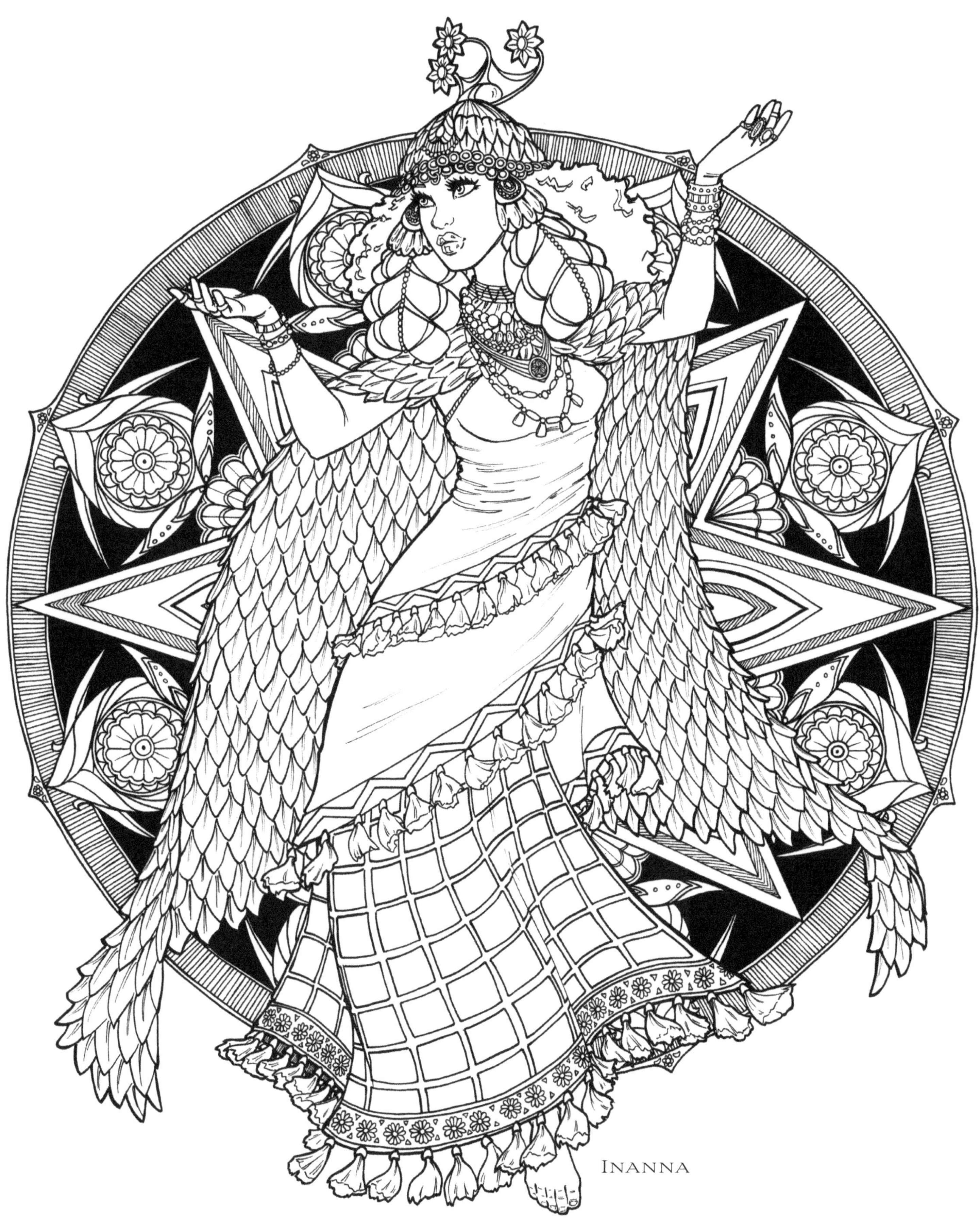

INANNA

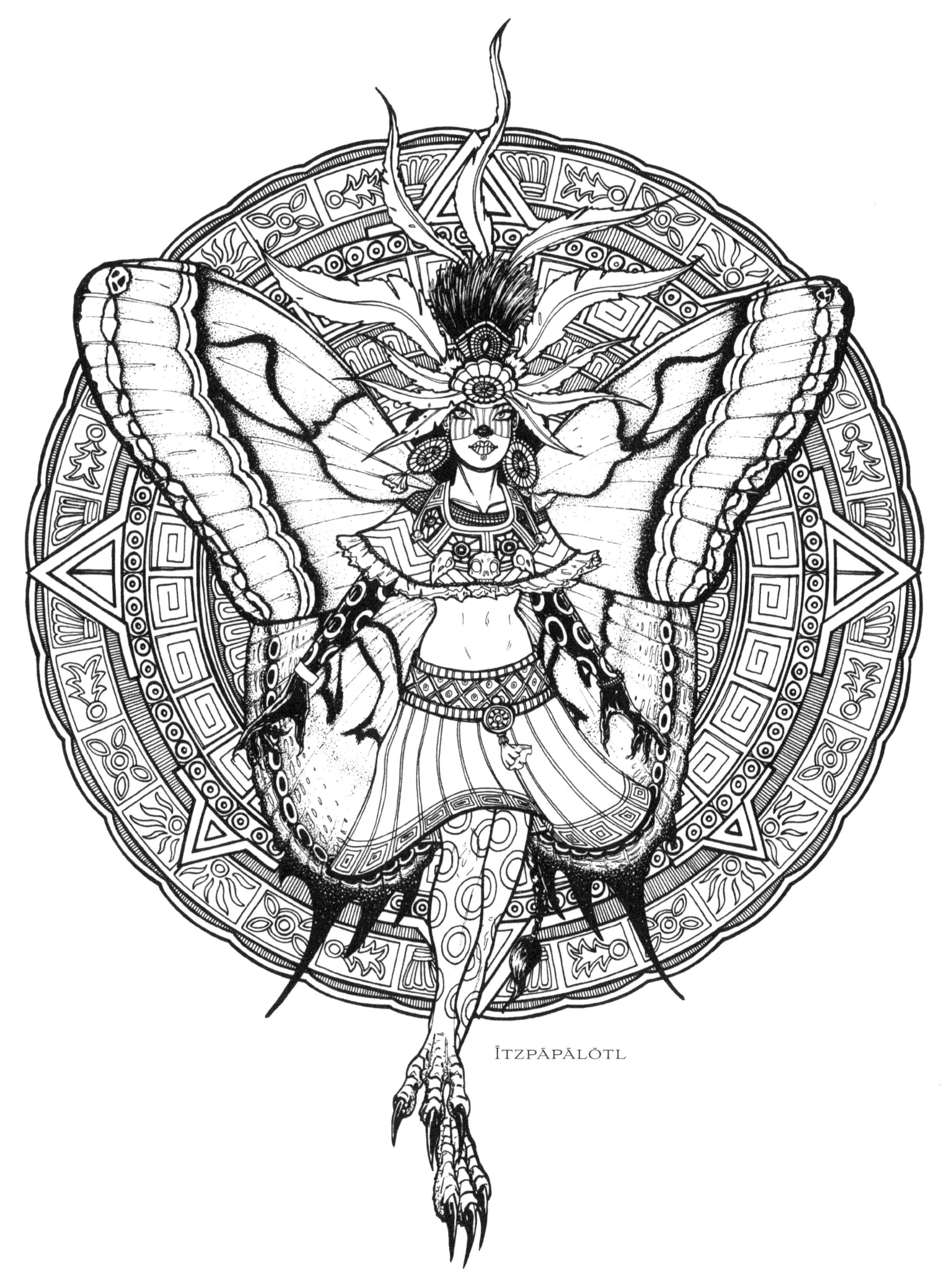
ĪTZPĀPĀLŌTL

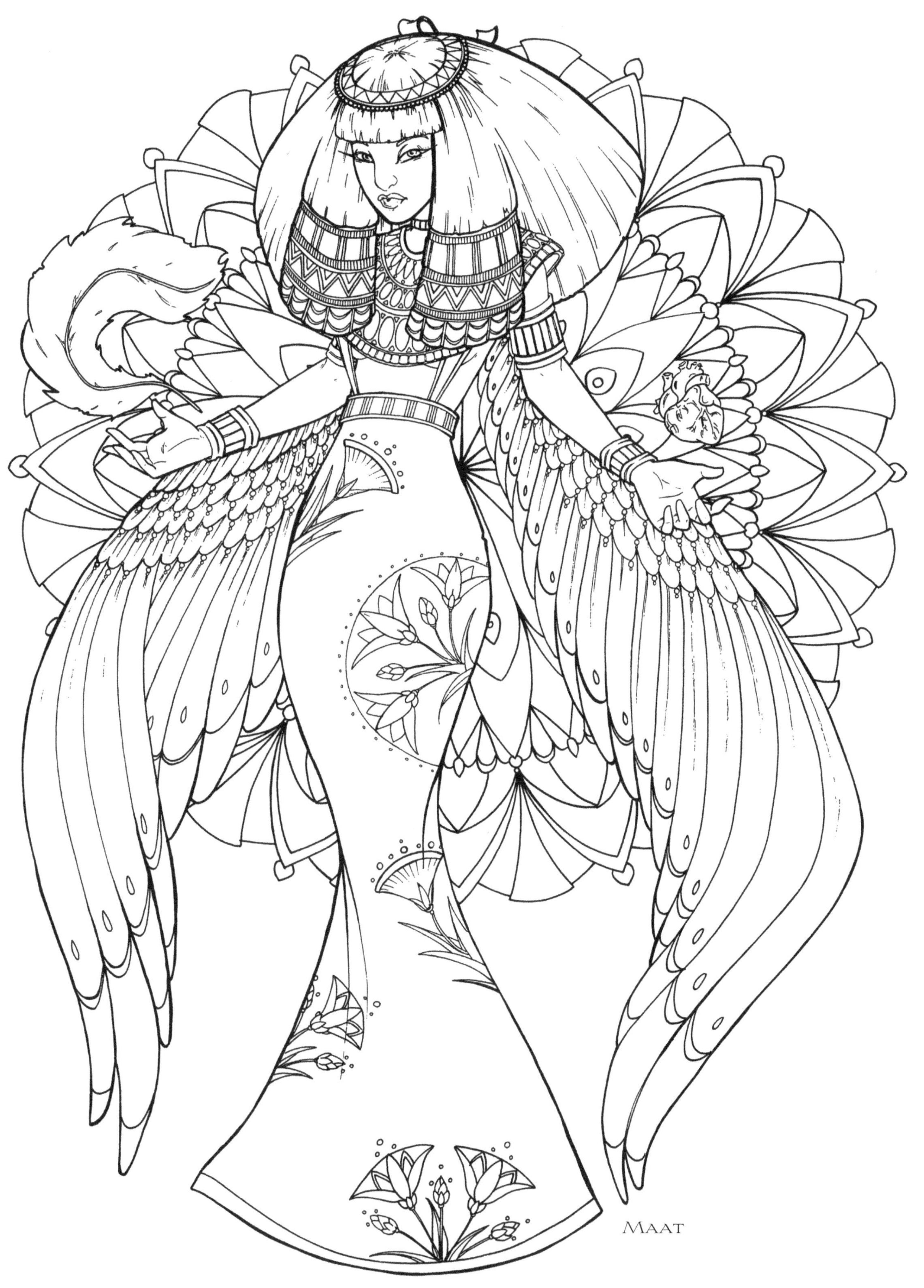
Maat

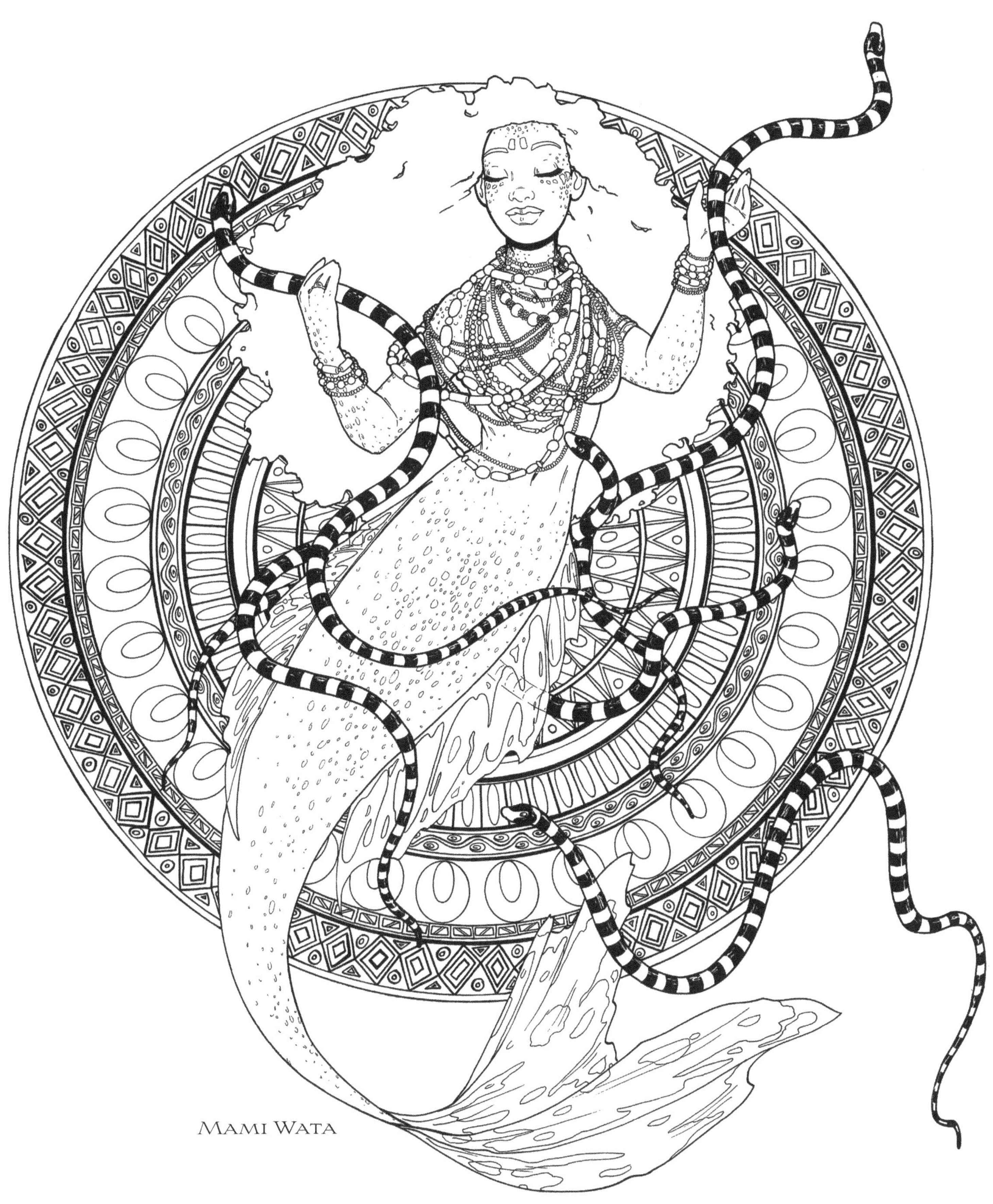

Mami Wata

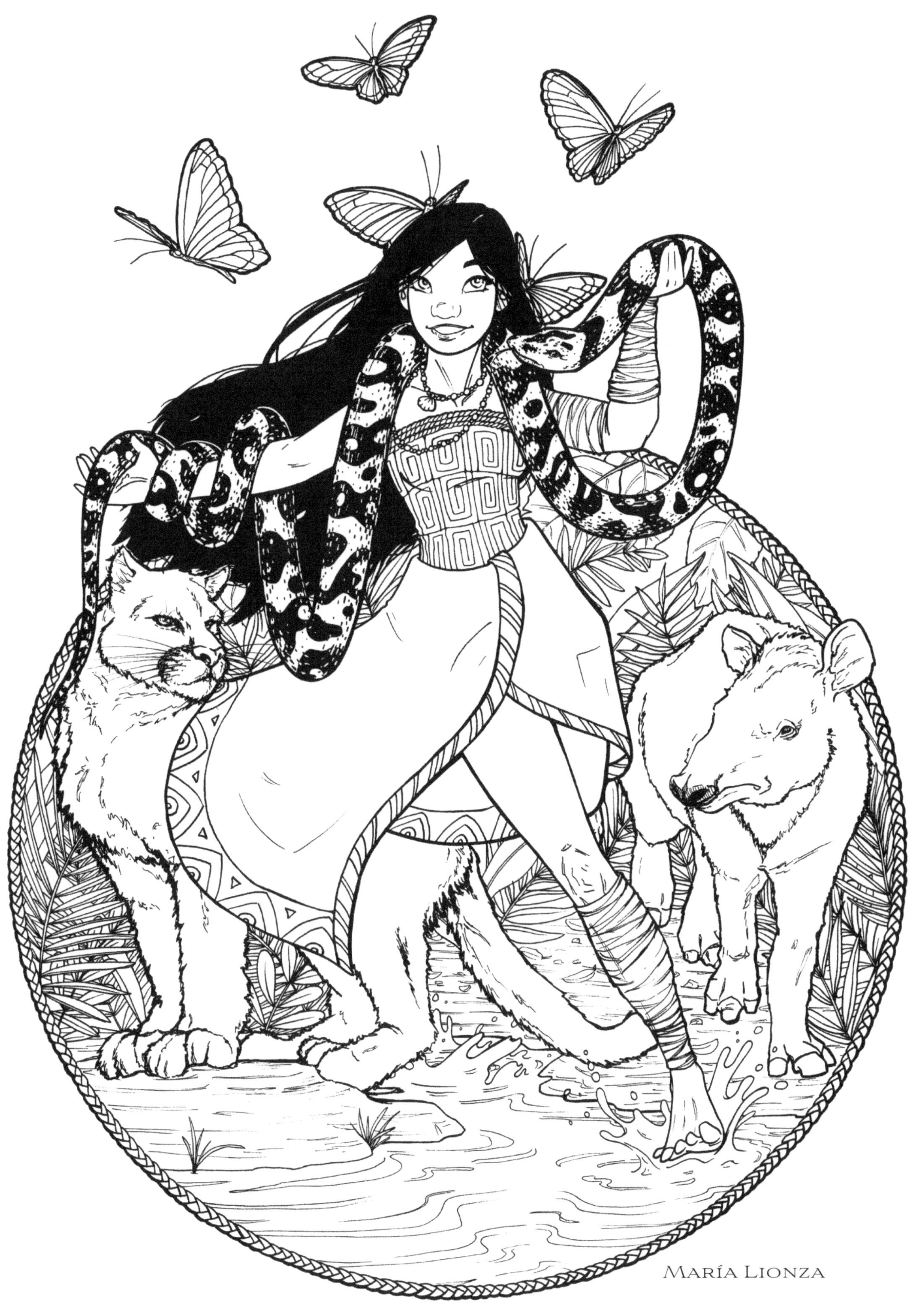

María Lionza

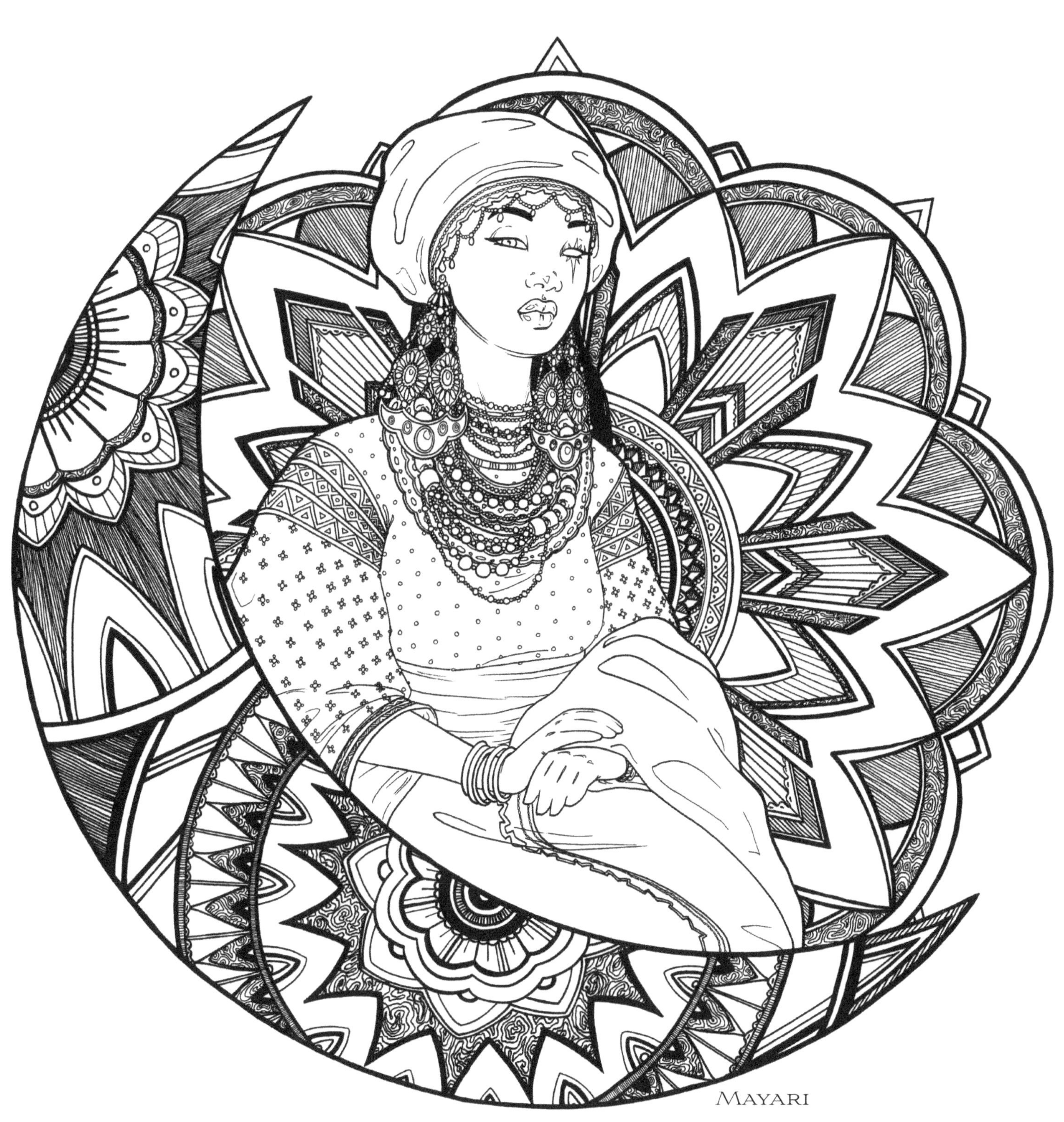

Mayari

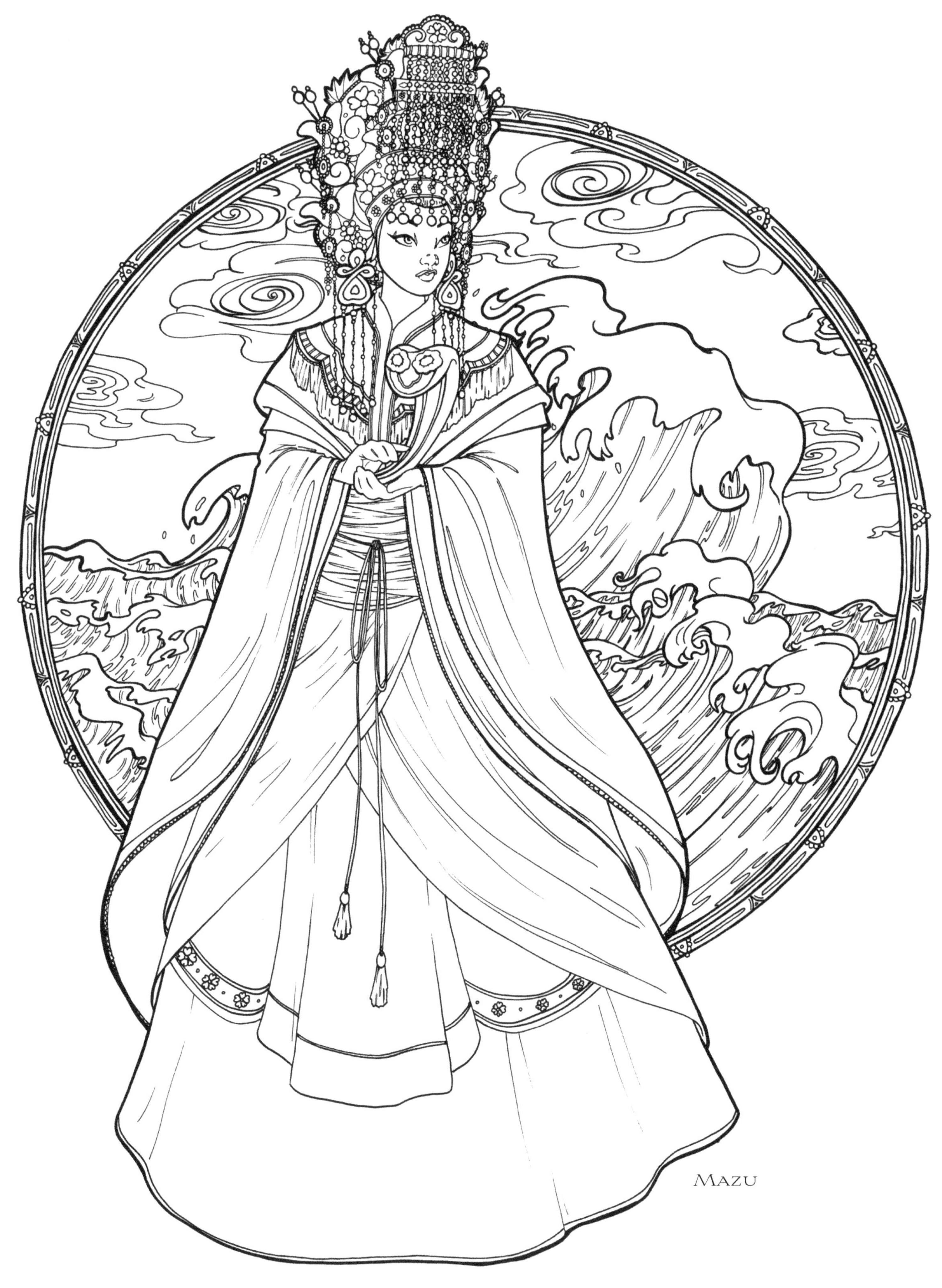
Mazu

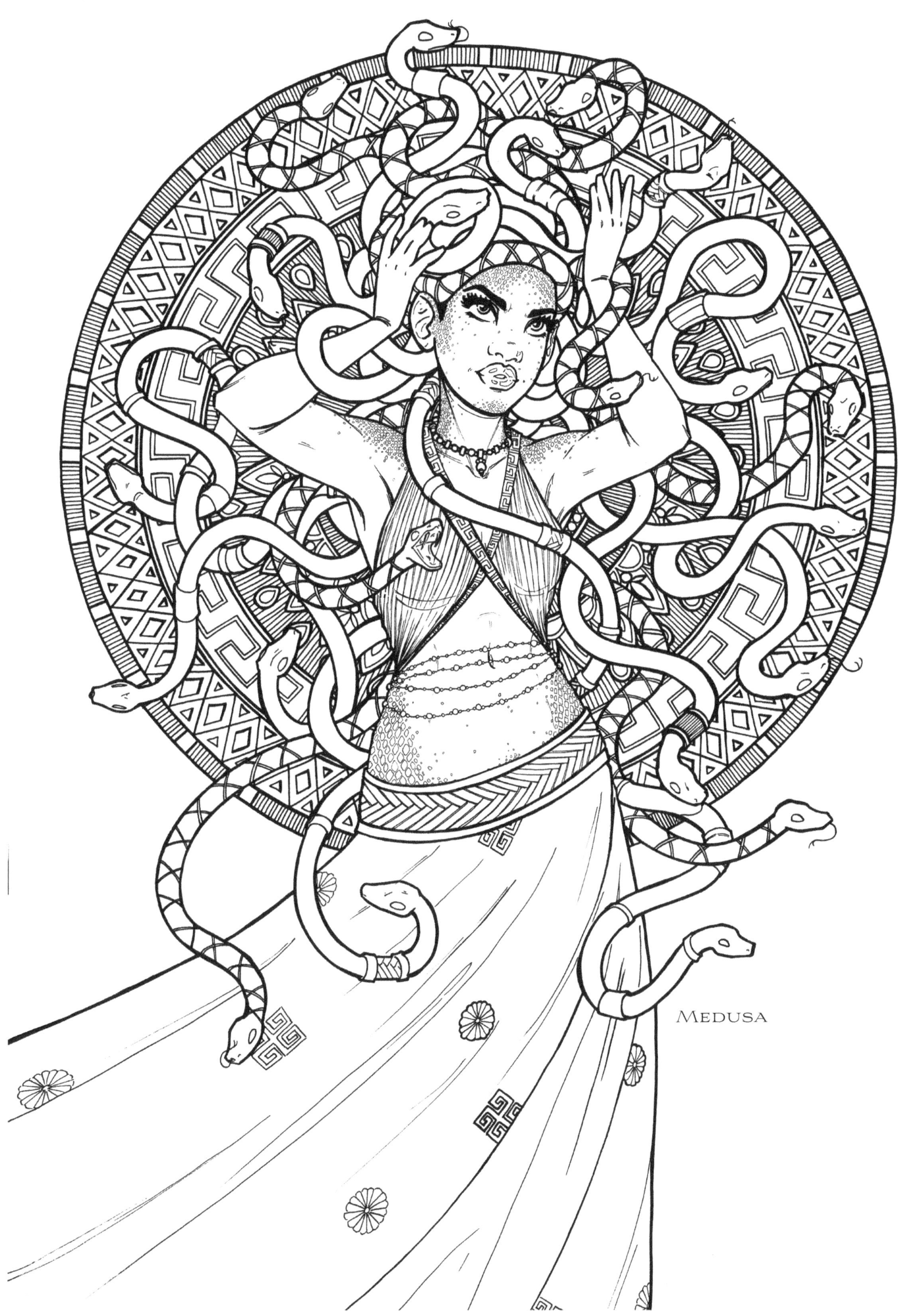

MEDUSA

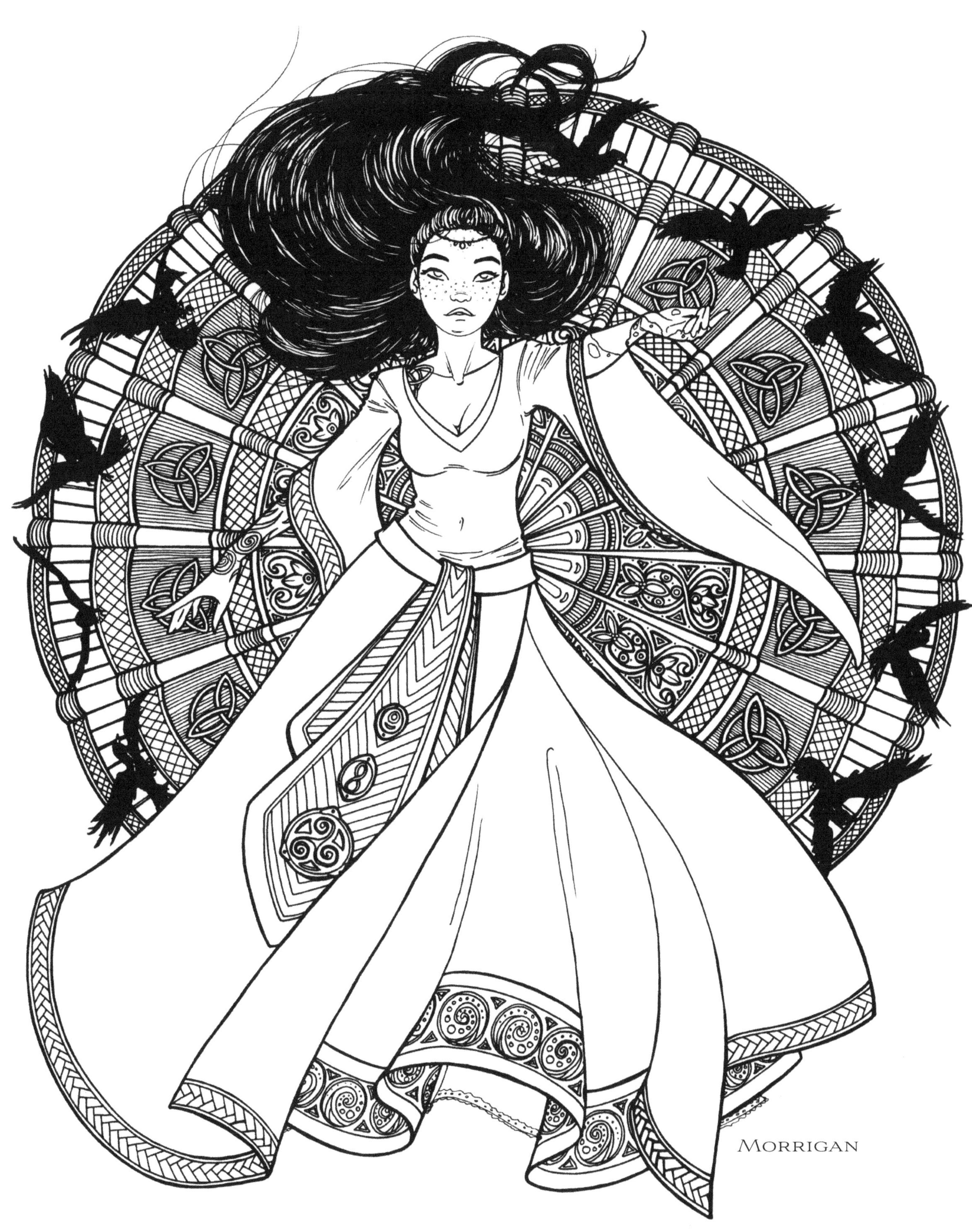

MORRIGAN

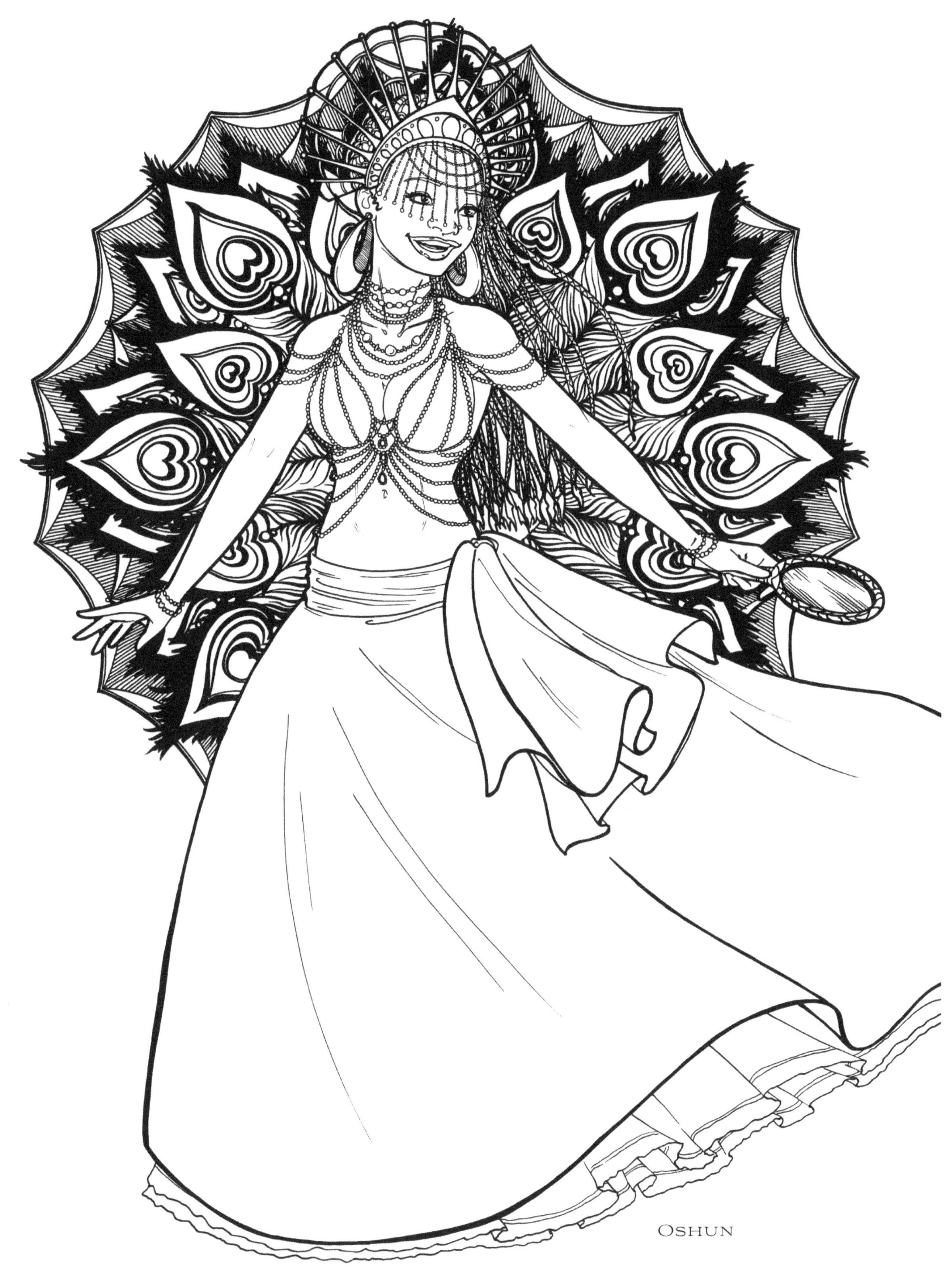
OSHUN

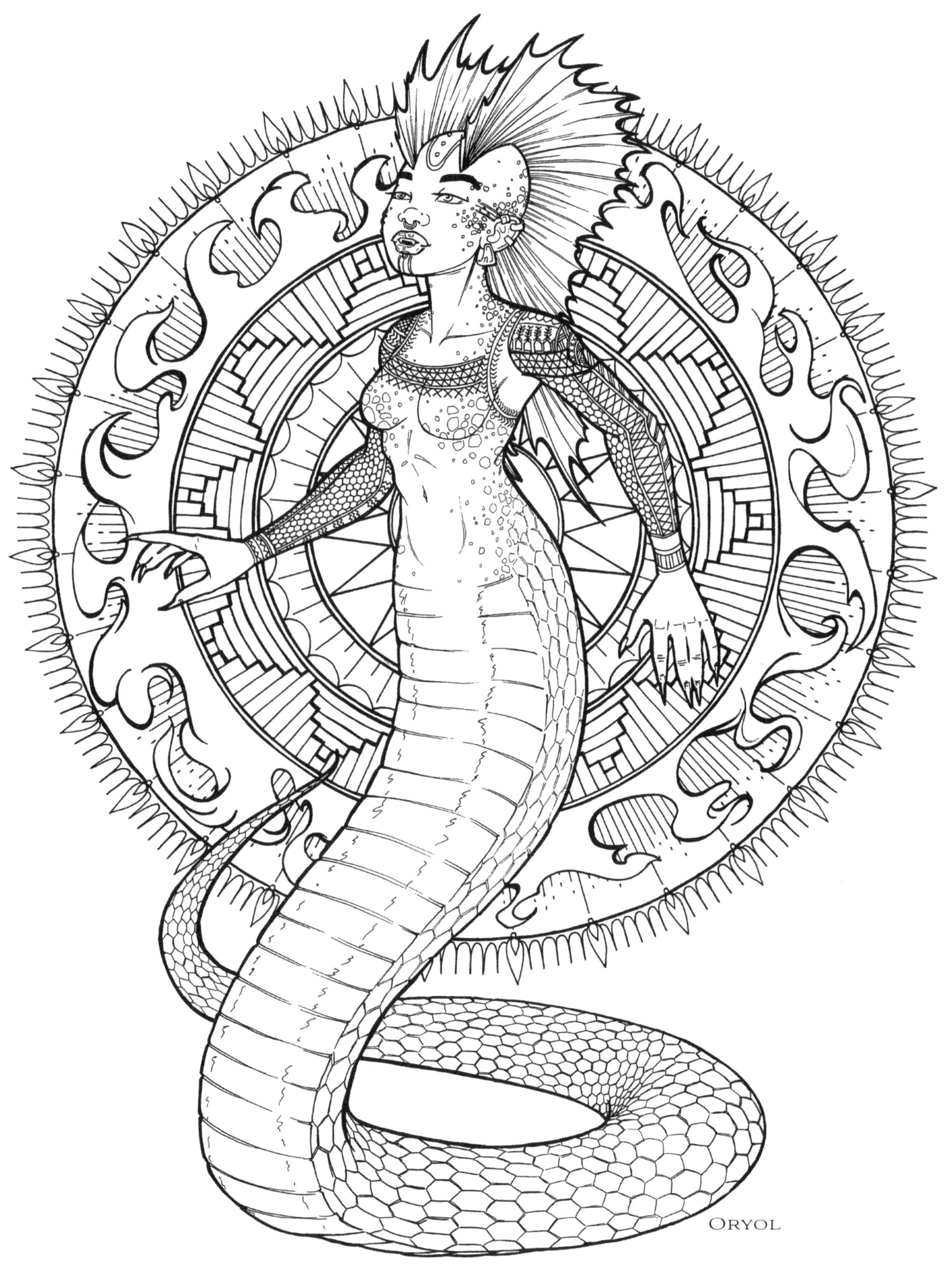
Oryol

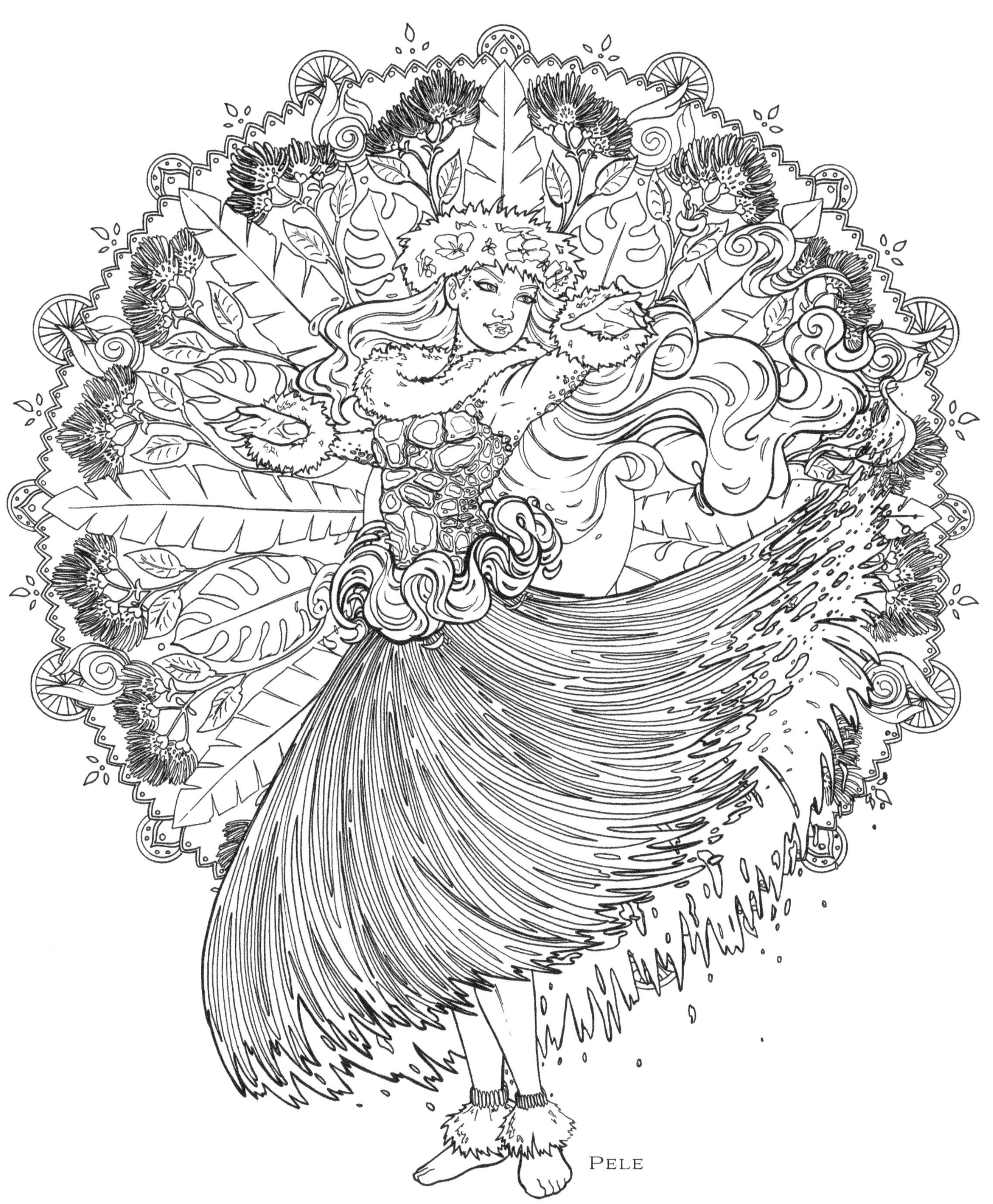
PELE

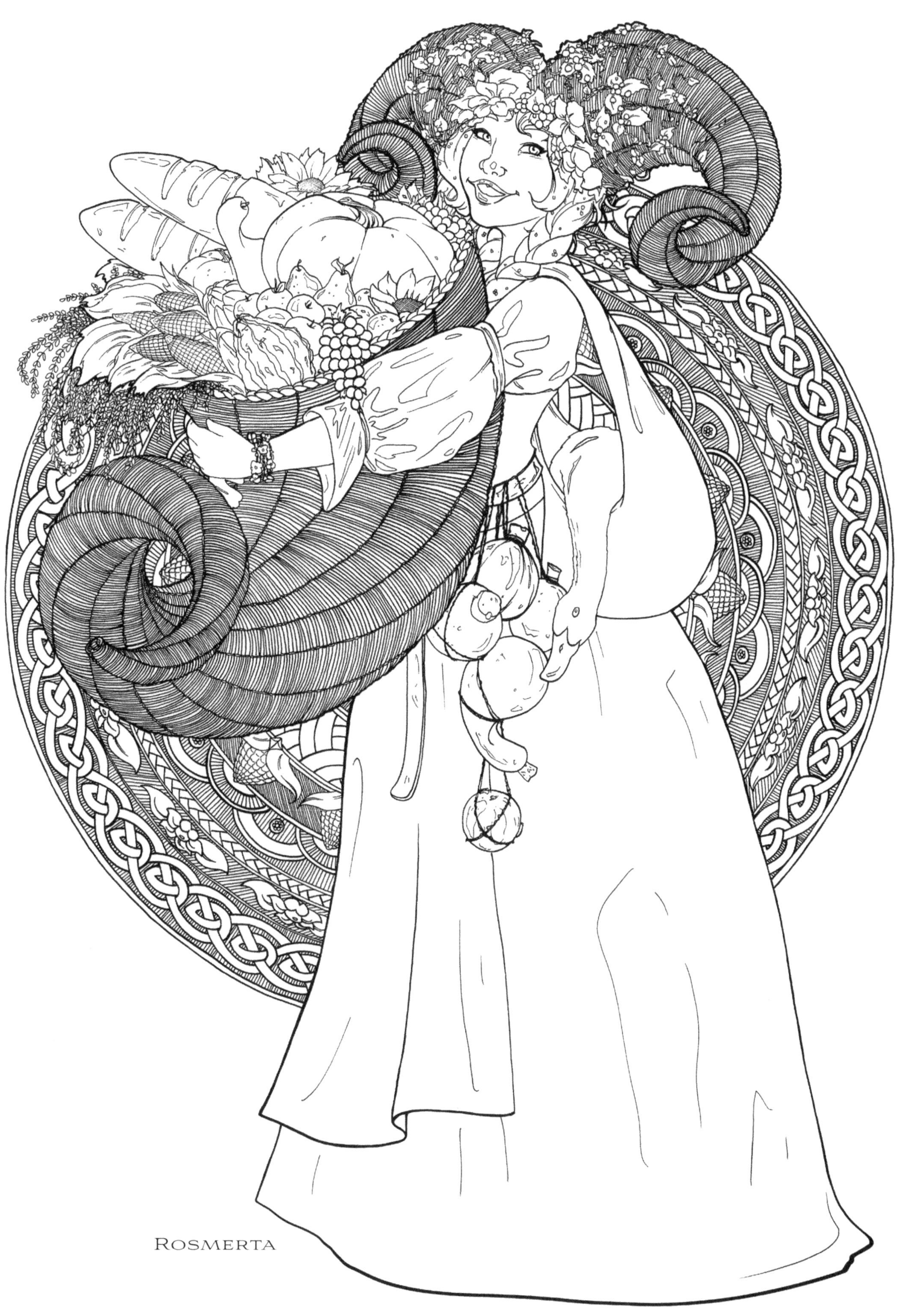

ROSMERTA

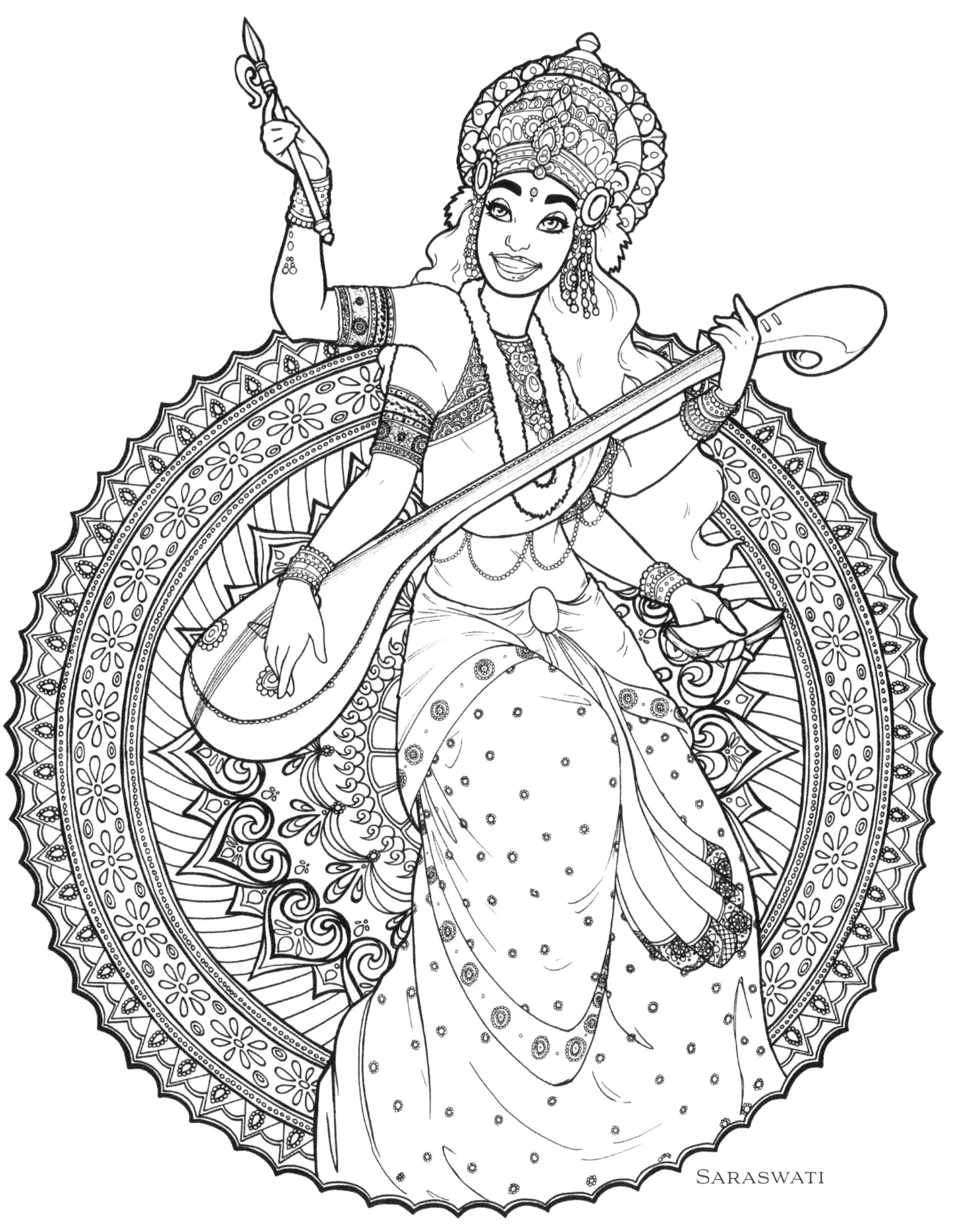

SARASWATI

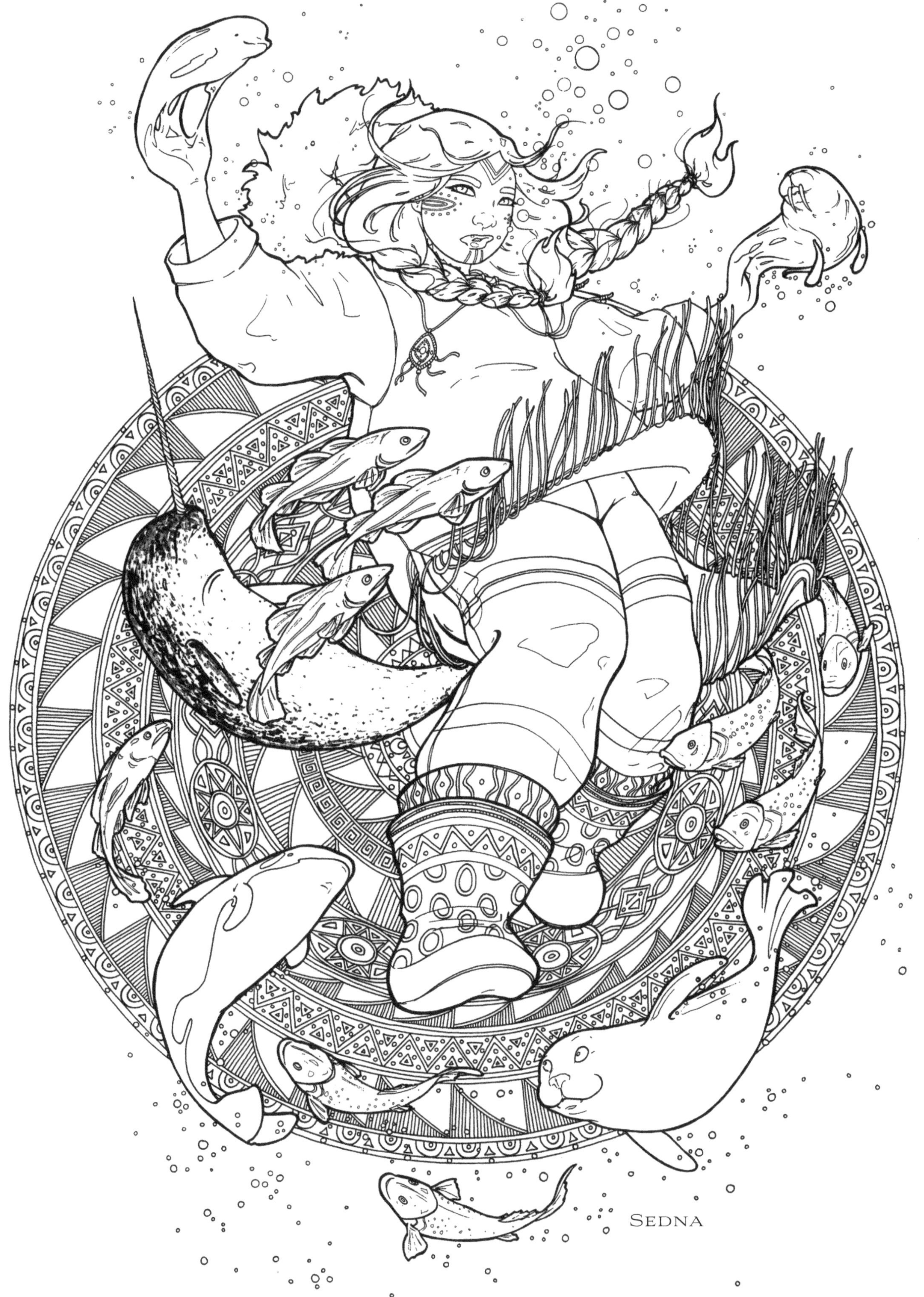
SEDNA

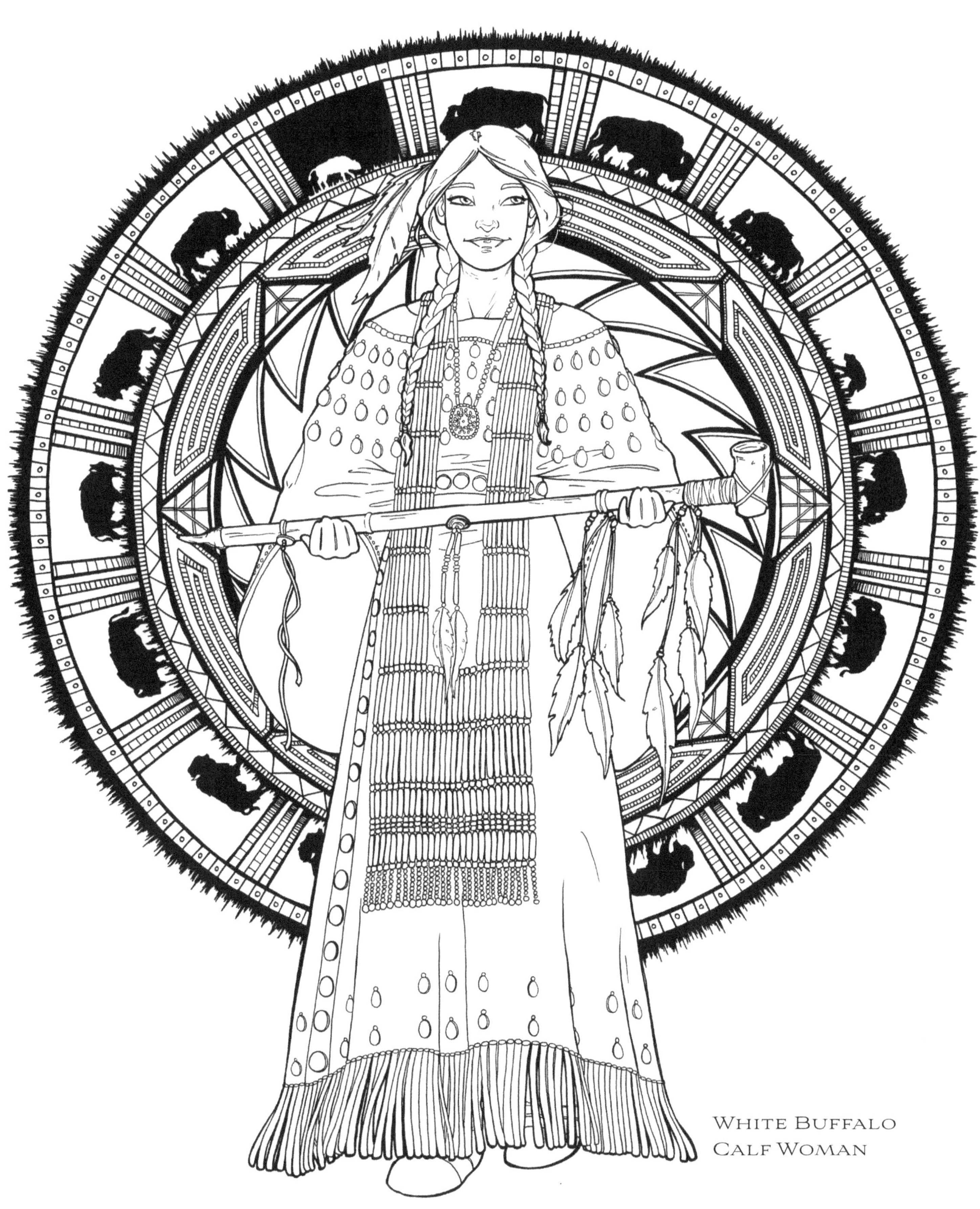

White Buffalo
Calf Woman

Index

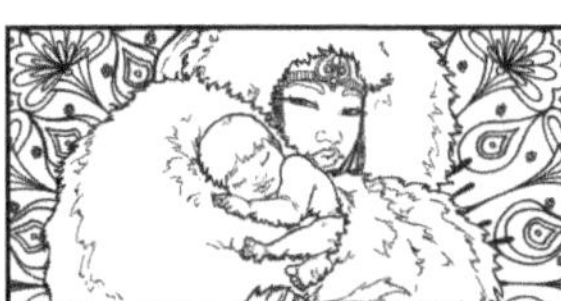 

Ajysyt

A Siberian fertility diety of the Yakut people who brings souls from heaven to be born, and records each one in the Golden Book of Fate. Women believe that by channeling Ajysyt they would be relieved of pain during childbirth. She is said to live on a mountaintop where she controls the fate of the world.

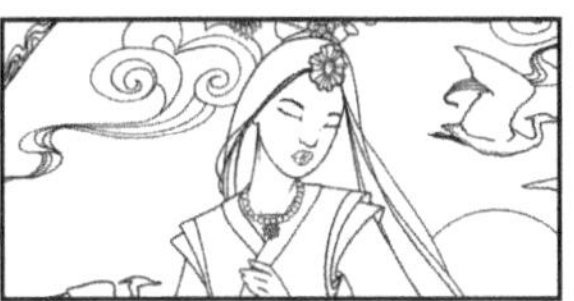 

Amaterasu

Also known as Amaterasu-Ōmikami or Ōhirume-no-Muchi-no-Kami, she is an embodiment of the rising sun and Japan itself. Central to the Shinto religion, Amaterasu is the daughter of creator deities Izanagi and Izanami, and has two siblings, the moon deity Tsukuyomi and the impetuous storm god Susanoo. She is considered to be one of the "Three Precious Children."

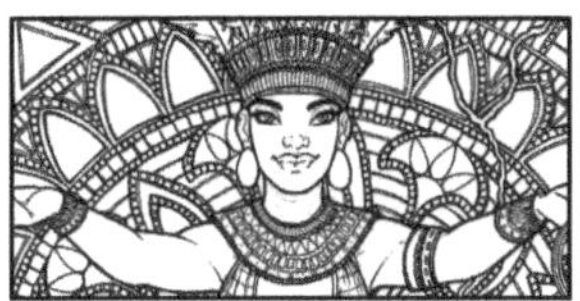 

Anuket

Originally a Nibian diety, Anuket is a personification of the Nile as "Nourisher of the Fields." She is also a goddess of the hunt and a protective deity during childbirth.

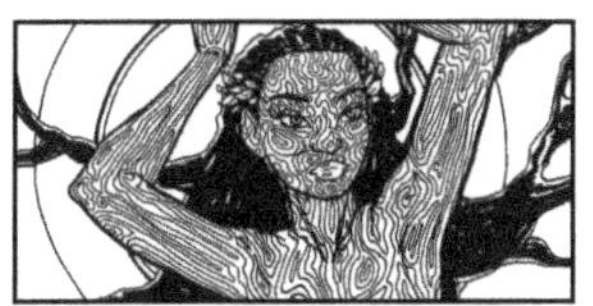 

Ashera

A major Semitic mother goddess and consort to God, appearing in multiple ancient texts. Other biblical references refer to her as a type of sacred pillar or tree that was erected next to Canaanite or Israelite altars, representing the divine feminine.

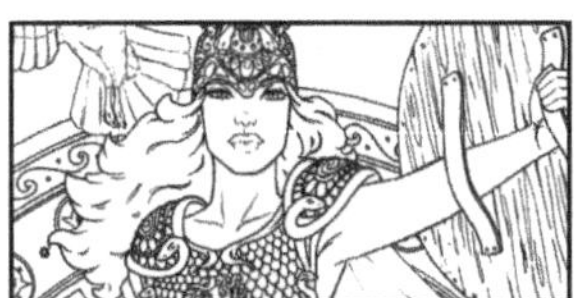 

Athena

The Greek goddess of wisdom, war, and – paradoxically – peace and handicrafts such as spinning and weaving. Symbols most associated with her include owls, olive trees, snakes, and the Gorgoneion. Majestic and stern, even Ares, the god of war, fears her. All Greek heroes ask her for help and advice.

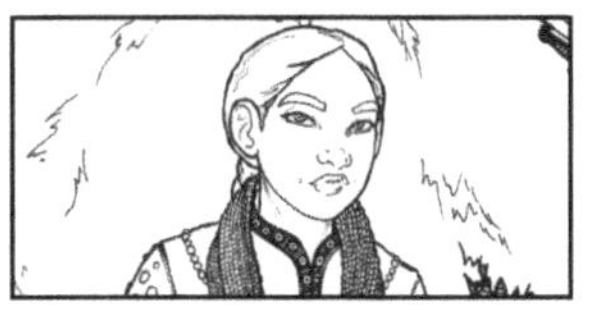 

Awasiûkiu (Mat'citiniu)

A bear of Menominee (Mamaceqtaw) Native folklore who fell in love with a human man, took the shape of a woman to be with him and they started a family together. During an unexpected visit from his relatives they saw her as a bear and attacked her, leaving her wounded at the shoulder. After learning who she was, they accepted her and called her Mat'citiniu (scar-shoulder woman).

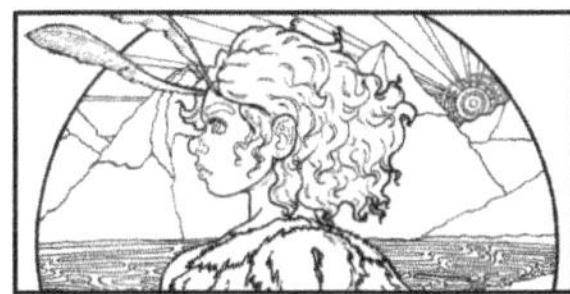 

Myee, Bogong Moth Woman

A figure of Australian Aboriginal lore who had colorful rainbow wings. In exploring a distant white mountain, snow fell, trapping her for the season. Eventually she was freed in the spring thaw, but as the ice melted from her wings, so too did her bright colors, leaving her wings an earthy brown. Soaking into the earth, the colors re-emerged as vibrant flowers.

Index (cont.)

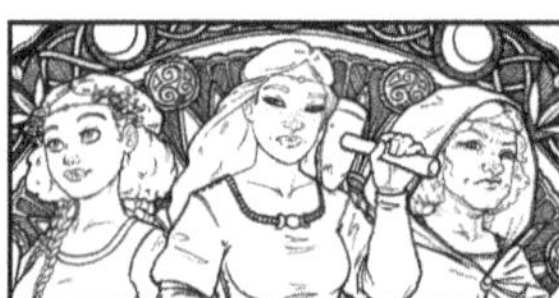  ### Brigid
An Irish triple goddess associated with wisdom, poetry, healing, protection, blacksmithing, and domesticated animals. She is tied to the Christian Saint Brigid, and is celebrated in the festival of Imbolc, which marks the beginning of spring.

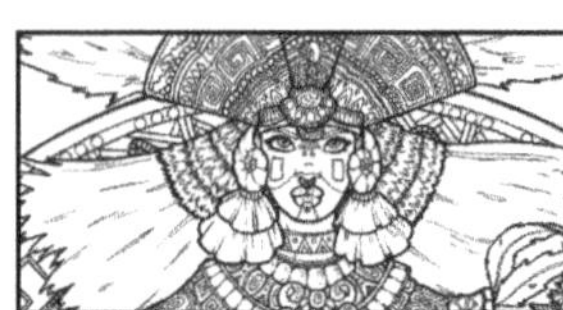  ### Chalchiuhtlicue
The Aztec goddess of flowing water as it collects on the earth, such as rivers, oceans, springs, and lakes. She was also the patroness of navigation, and a protector of childbirth and newborns, and responsible for the timely arrival of the water necessary for a successful harvest. Her name means "She of the Jade Skirt."

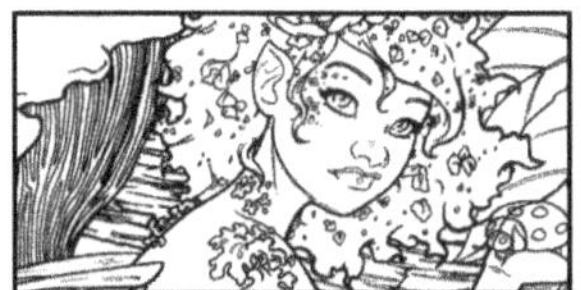  ### Damara
The Celtic Goddess of Children and Fertility, a Faerie Princess of the British Isles, and protector of children and the inner child. She is associated with the month of May and the festival of Beltane.

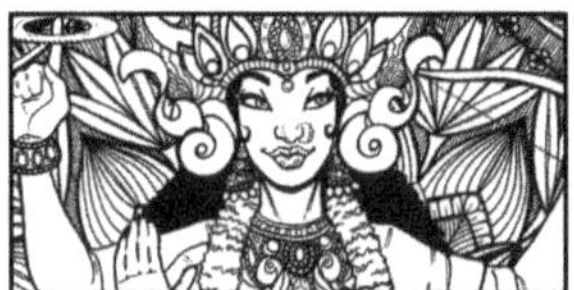  ### Durga
The goddess of protection, strength, motherhood, destruction, and wars, Durga was a major deity in Hinduism. She is known for unleashing her divine wrath against the wicked for the liberation of the oppressed, and entails destruction to empower creation.

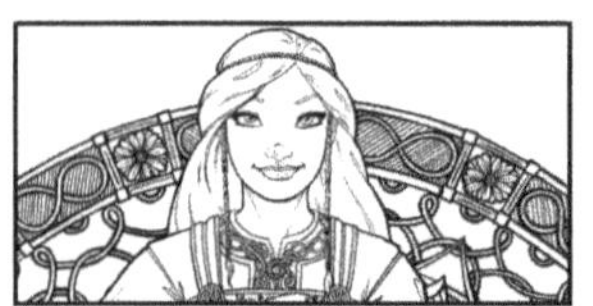  ### Eir
A goddess and handmaiden of Frigga in Norse mythology, as well as a valkyrie associated with healing and medicine. Her name signifies "peacefulness" and "mercy."

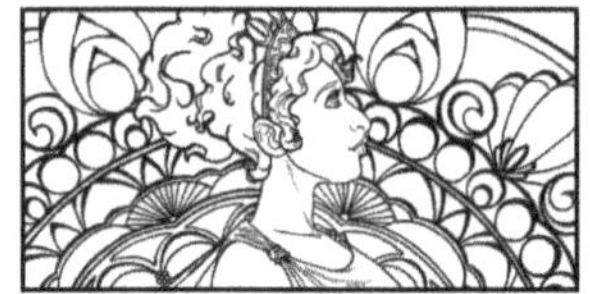  ### Gaia
Within Greek mythology Gaia is the personification of the Earth, and progenitor of all life. She is the mother of Uranus (the sky), as well as of Pontus (the sea).

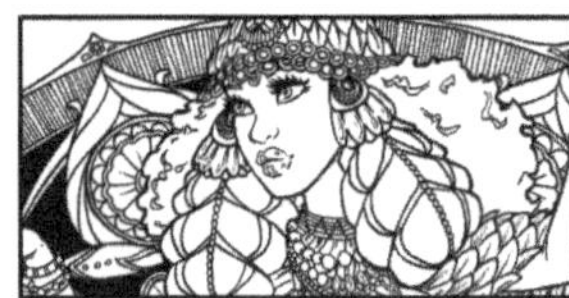  ### Inanna
Ancient Mesopotamian goddess associated with love, beauty, sex, war, justice, and political power. She was first worshipped in Sumer and was one of the most widely venerated deities in the Sumerian pantheon. Later she was worshipped by the Akkadians, Babylonians, and Assyrians as Ishtar.

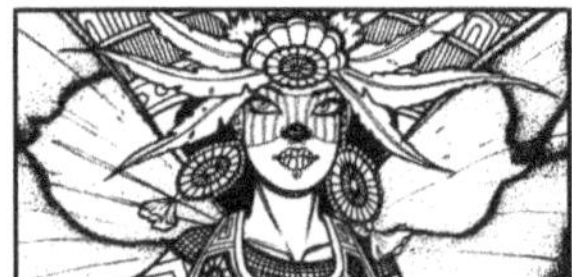  ### Ītzpāpālōtl
An Aztec warrior goddess who ruled over the world of Tamoanchan: the paradise of victims of infant mortality and the place where humans were created. Her name, meaning "clawed, obsidian butterfly," she could appear either in the form of a beautiful, seductive woman or terrifying goddess with a skeletal head and butterfly wings tipped with obsidian blades.

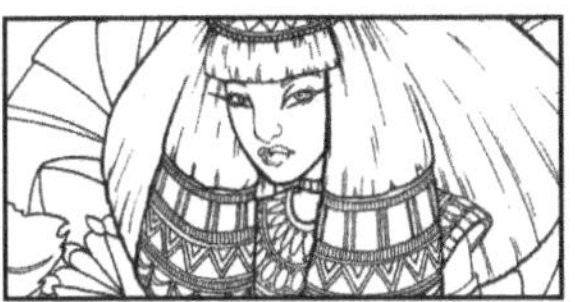 

Maat

The Egyptian personification of truth, justice, and the cosmic order. Her primary role deals with the Weighing of the Heart. Her feather was the measure that determined whether the souls would reach the paradise of the afterlife successfully. A heart that was heavier than the feather was deemed unworthy and fed to the demoness goddess Ammit.

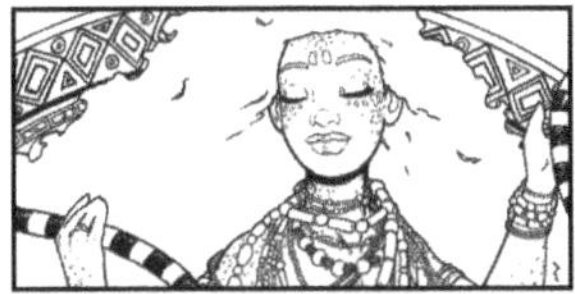 

Mami Wata

A water spirit often depicted as a mermaid but can also appear in human form. Patronage includes the sea, the moon, divination, healing, luck, money, and music. She is venerated in West African Vodun, Haitian Vodou, Folk Catholicism and the Yorùbá religion.

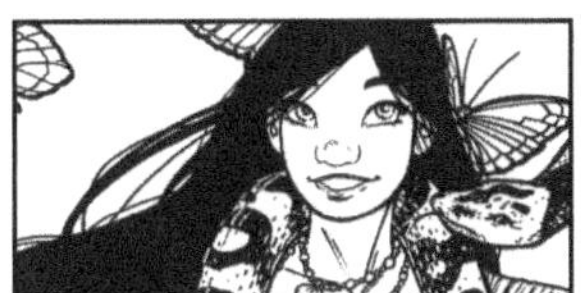 

María Lionza

The Venezuelan goddess of nature, love, peace, and harmony. In life she was the daughter of an indigenous chief. After being sent to live in the Sorte Mountain, María Lionza was attacked by the Great Anaconda. Begging Sorte Mountain for help, she then disintegrated and merged with the mountain.

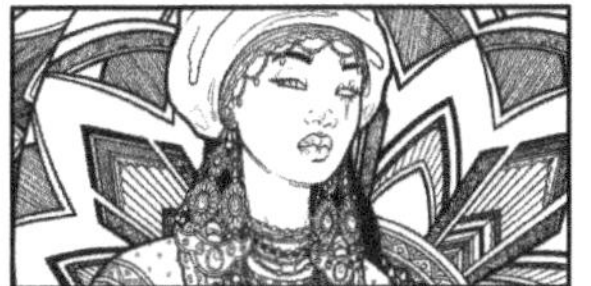 

Mayari

The Philippine goddess of the moon, combat, beauty, revolution, equality, and strength. After the death of their father, Mayari fought her brother, Apolaki, as he wanted to rule alone and she wanted equal rule of the skies. In combat, she lost her eye and out of guilt he conceded to equal rule at different times. Because of the loss of her eye, her light is dimmer.

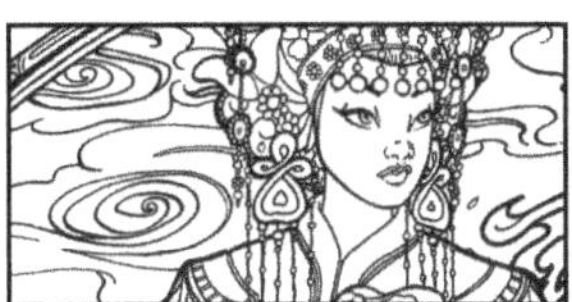 

Mazu

A Chinese goddess who was revered as a patron deity of seafarers, such as fishermen and sailors. She now is regarded by her believers as a powerful and benevolent Queen of Heaven. In life, she was Lin Mo or Lin Moniang, a Fujianese shamaness who possessed the uncanny ability to predict weather, and would often rescue people from the sea, even in the harshest conditions.

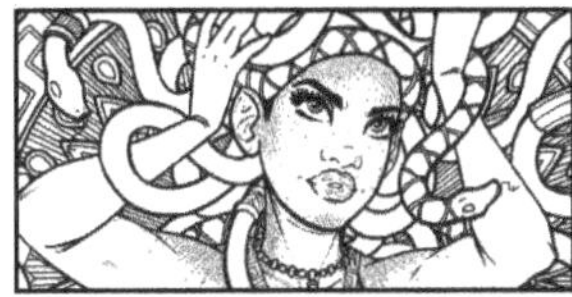 

Medusa

One of three Gorgon sisters in Greek Mythology who had living venomous snakes in place of hair, she also had the power to turn those who gazed upon her into stone. Over time her story has evolved and she has since become the symbol of protection, beauty, and feminine rage against those seeking to demonize female authority.

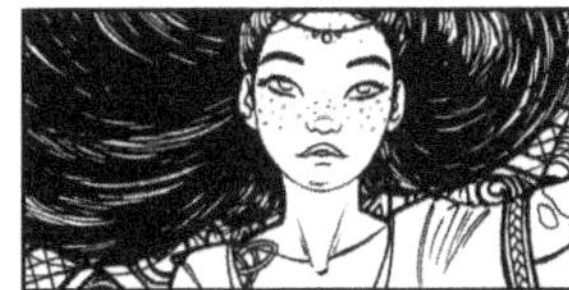 

The Morrigan

The Irish goddess of war and fate, she often appears as a crow, inciting warriors to bravery and battle. It has also been said that she can sometimes be seen before battle, washing the blood-stained clothes of those warriors fated to die.

Index (cont.)

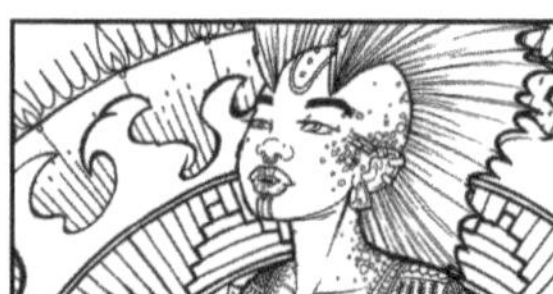 

Oryol

A Philippine demi-goddess who possesses inhuman beauty and seductive prowess along with an enchanting voice that could lure any living creature be it human or animal. In one tale, she was cursed by a jealous spirit who turned her into a serpent woman, becoming a guardian of the forest.

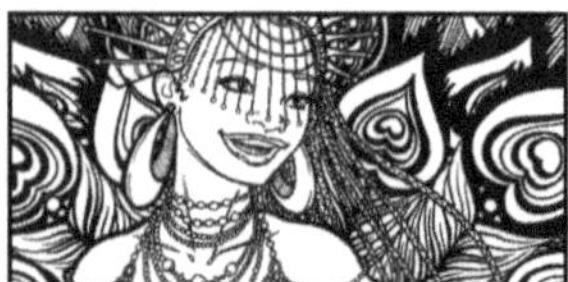 

Oshun

An orisha (goddess) of West Africa associated with water, purity, fertility, love, and sensuality. She is the most prominent and venerated of all the Orishas, connected to destiny and divination. Oshun is also an important river deity among the Yorùbá people, as well as the patron saint of the Osun River in Nigeria, which bears her name.

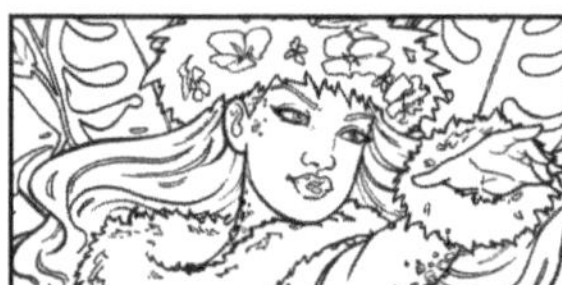 

Pele

Also referred to as "Madame Pele" or "Tūtū Pele" as a sign of respect, she is the goddess of volcanoes, fire, and the creator of the Hawai'ian Islands. Pele is one of the most well known deities of the Hawai'ian Islands. She is also regarded as the goddess of the hula and is known as "She who shapes the sacred land," in ancient Hawai'ian chants.

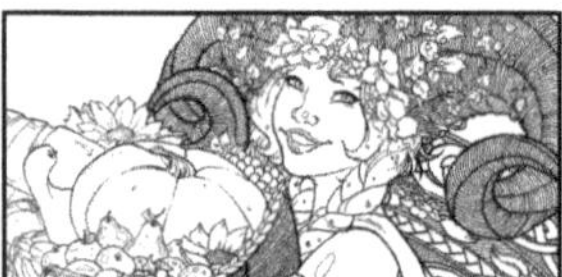 

Rosmerta

The Great Provider, a Celtic and Gallo-Roman Goddess of abundance, fertility, and wealth. She is celebrated in the festival of Lughnasadh, or Lammas, often depicted carrying a cornucopia and/or a basket of fruit, symbolizing abundance. In the Roman pantheon she is sometimes associated with Mercury and healing.

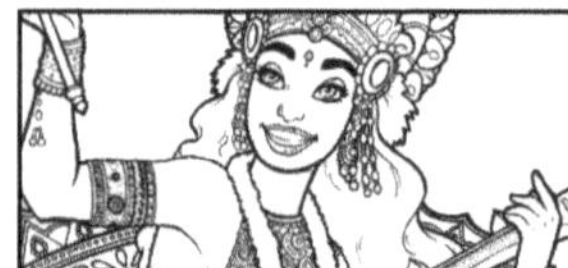 

Saraswati

The Hindu goddess of education, creativity, and music. She endows human beings with speech and wisdom. Her four hands represent aspects of human personality in learning: mind, intellect, alertness, and ego. In some interpretations, "Sara" is translated as meaning "Essence," and "Sva" is translated as meaning "Self," which together translate to meaning "She who helps realize the essence of one's self."

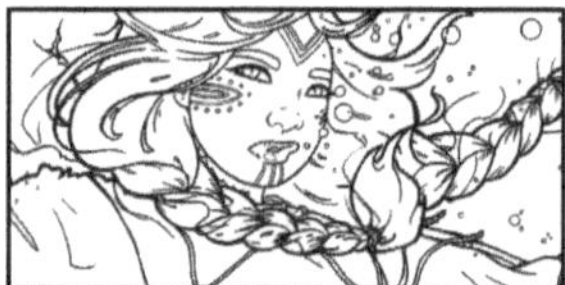 

Sedna

The Inuit goddess of the sea and the underworld. In each version of her legend, her father took her to sea and threw her from his kayak, chopping off her fingers when she tried to climb back. She sank to the bottom of the sea, her disembodied fingers turning into sea creatures. Hunters must placate and pray to her to release the sea animals from the depths for their hunt.

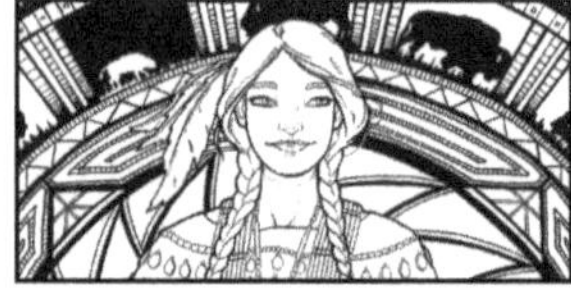 

White Buffalo Calf Woman

A sacred woman of a supernatural origin who came to the Lakota people at a desperate time in their history, bringing them instructions for balance, harmony, abundance, and hope.

*For more info on these goddesses use the QR links provided or look up their stories at Wikipedia, journeyingtothegoddess.wordpress.com, nativesymbols.info, and aswangproject.com. You can also check out the book "Encyclopedia of Goddesses and Heroines" by Patricia Monaghan.